Formation of the Earth, Grade 9

What if you could challenge your ninth graders to use geologic theory and standards of measurement to explore different epochs and time periods of the Earth's formation? With this volume in the *STEM Road Map Curriculum Series*, you can!

Formation of the Earth outlines a journey that will steer your students toward authentic problem solving while grounding them in integrated STEM disciplines. Like the other volumes in the series, this book is designed to meet the growing need to infuse real-world learning into K–12 classrooms.

This interdisciplinary, three-lesson module uses project- and problem-based learning to help students investigate how Earth science professionals gather information and develop theories about the formation of the Earth and the processes taking place since the proliferation of humans. Working in teams, students will work to identify, define and describe the attributes scientists use to delineate Earth's eras, periods, and epochs, in order to determine the appropriate boundary event to define the Anthropocene Epoch, and will develop a publication-ready textbook entry for an Earth science textbook. To support this goal, students will do the following:

- Identify, define, and describe attributes of eras, periods, and epochs which have marked geologic time in Earth's history.

- Evaluate various possible index layers and boundary events that mark the beginning of the Anthropocene Epoch to determine which is most appropriate when labeling the current epoch in Earth's history.

- Design and present a multimedia presentation to share with textbook publishers regarding information on the Anthropocene Epoch, to include in a secondary-level Earth science textbook.

- Create a publication-ready textbook entry describing the Anthropocene Epoch.

The *STEM Road Map Curriculum Series* is anchored in the Next Generation Science Standards, the Common Core State Standards, and the Framework for 21st Century Learning. In-depth and flexible, *Formation of the Earth* can be used as a whole unit or in part to meet the needs of districts, schools, and teachers who are charting a course toward an integrated STEM approach.

Carla C. Johnson is Professor of Science Education in the College of Education and Office of Research and Innovation, and a Faculty Research Fellow at North Carolina State University in North Carolina, USA

Janet B. Walton is Senior Research Scholar at North Carolina State University in North Carolina, USA

Erin E. Peters-Burton is the Donna R. and David E. Sterling Endowed Professor in Science Education at George Mason University in Virginia, USA

STEM ROAD MAP CURRICULUM SERIES

Series editors: Carla C. Johnson, Janet B. Walton, and Erin E. Peters-Burton

Map out a journey that will steer your students toward authentic problem solving as you ground them in integrated STEM disciplines.

Co-published by Routledge and NSTA Press, in partnership with the National Science Teaching Association, this K–12 curriculum series is anchored in the Next Generation Science Standards, the Common Core State Standards, and the Framework for 21st Century Learning. It was developed to meet the growing need to infuse real-world STEM learning into classrooms.

Each book is an in-depth module that uses project- and problem-based learning. First, your students are presented with a challenge. Then, they apply what they learn using science, social studies, English language arts, and mathematics. Engaging and flexible, each volume can be used as a whole unit or in part to meet the needs of districts, schools, and teachers who are charting a course toward an integrated STEM approach.

Modules are available from NSTA Press and Routledge, and organized under the following themes. For an update listing of the volumes in the series, please visit https://www.routledge.com/STEM-Road-Map-Curriculum-Series/book-series/SRM (for titles co-published by Routledge and NSTA Press), or www.nsta.org/book-series/stem-road-map-curriculum (for titles published by NSTA Press).

Co-published by Routledge and NSTA Press:

Optimizing the Human Experience:

- *Our Changing Environment, Grade K: STEM Road Map for Elementary School*
- *Genetically Modified Organisms, Grade 7: STEM Road Map for Middle School*
- *Rebuilding the Natural Environment, Grade 10: STEM Road Map for High School*
- *Mineral Resources, Grade 11: STEM Road Map for High School*

Cause and Effect:

- *Formation of the Earth, Grade 9: STEM Road Map for High School*

Published by NSTA Press:

Innovation and Progress:

- *Amusement Park of the Future, Grade 6: STEM Road Map for Elementary School*
- *Transportation in the Future, Grade 3: STEM Road Map for Elementary School*
- *Harnessing Solar Energy, Grade 4: STEM Road Map for Elementary School*
- *Wind Energy, Grade 5: STEM Road Map for Elementary School*
- *Construction Materials, Grade 11: STEM Road Map for High School*

The Represented World:

- *Patterns and the Plant World, Grade 1: STEM Road Map for Elementary School*

- *Investigating Environmental Changes, Grade 2: STEM Road Map for Elementary School*
- *Swing Set Makeover, Grade 3: STEM Road Map for Elementary School*
- *Rainwater Analysis, Grade 5: STEM Road Map for Elementary School*
- *Packaging Design, Grade 6: STEM Road Map for Middle School*
- *Improving Bridge Design, Grade 8: STEM Road Map for Middle School*
- *Radioactivity, Grade 11: STEM Road Map for High School*
- *Car Crashes, Grade 12: STEM Road Map for High School*

Cause and Effect:

- *Physics in Motion, Grade K: STEM Road Map for Elementary School*
- *Influence of Waves, Grade 1: STEM Road Map for Elementary School*
- *Natural Hazards, Grade 2: STEM Road Map for Elementary School*
- *Human Impacts on Our Climate, Grade 6: STEM Road Map for Middle School*
- *The Changing Earth, Grade 8: STEM Road Map for Middle School*
- *Healthy Living, Grade 10: STEM Road Map for High School*

Formation of the Earth

Grade
9

STEM Road Map for High School

Edited by Carla C. Johnson, Janet B. Walton, and
Erin E. Peters-Burton

NEW YORK AND LONDON

Cover images: icon © Shutterstock, map © Getty Images
Art and design for cover and interior adapted from NSTA Press

First published 2022
by Routledge
605 Third Avenue, New York, NY 10158

and by Routledge
4 Park Square, Milton Park, Abingdon, Oxon, OX14 4RN

Routledge is an imprint of the Taylor & Francis Group, an informa business

A co-publication with NSTA Press.

Library of Congress Cataloging-in-Publication Data
Names: Johnson, Carla C., 1969– editor. | Walton, Janet B., 1968– editor. | Peters-Burton, Erin E., editor.
Title: Formation of the earth, grade 9 : STEM road map for high school / edited by Carla C. Johnson, Janet B. Walton, and Erin E. Peters-Burton.
Description: New York, NY : Routledge, 2022. | Series: STEM road map curriculum series | Includes bibliographical references and index.
Identifiers: LCCN 2021053361 | ISBN 9781032199917 (hardback) | ISBN 9781032199900 (paperback) | ISBN 9781003261766 (ebook)
Subjects: LCSH: Earth sciences—Study and teaching (Secondary) | Formations (Geology)—Study and teaching (Secondary)
Classification: LCC QE40 .F67 2022 | DDC 550.71/2—dc23/eng/20211223
LC record available at https://lccn.loc.gov/2021053361

ISBN: 978-1-032-19991-7 (hbk)
ISBN: 978-1-032-19990-0 (pbk)
ISBN: 978-1-003-26176-6 (ebk)

DOI: 10.4324/9781003261766

Typeset in Palatino LT Std
by Apex CoVantage, LLC

CONTENTS

Part 1: The STEM Road Map: Background, Theory, and Practice

Part 2: Formation of the Earth: STEM Road Map Module

CONTENTS

ABOUT THE EDITORS
AND AUTHORS

Dr. Carla C. Johnson is a Professor of Science Education and ORI Faculty Research Fellow at NC State University in Raleigh, North Carolina. Dr. Johnson served as the director of research and evaluation for the Department of Defense–funded Army Educational Outreach Program (AEOP), a global portfolio of STEM education programs, competitions, and apprenticeships. She has been a leader in STEM education for the past decade, serving as the director of STEM Centers, editor of the *School Science and Mathematics* journal, and lead researcher for the evaluation of Tennessee's Race to the Top–funded STEM portfolio. Dr. Johnson has published over 100 articles, books, book chapters, and curriculum books focused on STEM education. She is a former science and social studies teacher and was the recipient of the 2013 Outstanding Science Teacher Educator of the Year award from the Association for Science Teacher Education (ASTE), the 2012 Award for Excellence in Integrating Science and Mathematics from the School Science and Mathematics Association (SSMA), the 2014 award for best paper on Implications of Research for Educational Practice from ASTE, and the 2006 Outstanding Early Career Scholar Award from SSMA. Her research focuses on STEM education policy implementation, effective science teaching, and integrated STEM approaches.

Dr. Janet B. Walton is a Senior Research Scholar at NC State's College of Education in Raleigh, North Carolina. Formerly the STEM workforce program manager for Virginia's Region 2000 and founding director of the Future Focus Foundation, a nonprofit organization dedicated to enhancing the quality of STEM education in the region, she merges her economic development and education backgrounds to develop K–12 curricular materials that integrate real-life issues with sound cross-curricular content. Her research focus includes collaboration between schools and community stakeholders for STEM education, problem- and project- based learning pedagogies, online learning, and mixed methods research methodologies. She leverages this background to bring contextual STEM experiences into the classroom and provide students and educators with innovative resources and curricular materials. She is the former assistant director of evaluation of research and evaluation for the Department of Defense–funded Army Educational Outreach Program (AEOP), a global portfolio of STEM education programs, competitions, and apprenticeships and specializes in evaluation of STEM programs.

Dr. Erin E. Peters-Burton is the Donna R. and David E. Sterling Endowed Professor in Science Education at George Mason University in Fairfax, Virginia. She uses her experiences from 15 years as an engineer and secondary science, engineering, and mathematics teacher to develop research projects that directly inform classroom practice in science and engineering. Her research agenda is based on the idea that all students should build self-awareness of how they learn science and engineering. She works to help students see themselves as "science- minded" and help teachers create classrooms that support student skills to develop scientific knowledge. To accomplish this, she pursues research projects that investigate ways that students and teachers can use self-regulated learning theory in science and engineering, as well as how inclusive STEM schools can help students succeed. She received the Outstanding Science Teacher Educator of the Year award from ASTE in 2016 and a Teacher of Distinction Award and a Scholarly Achievement Award from George Mason University in 2012, and in 2010 she was named University Science Educator of the Year by the Virginia Association of Science Teachers.

Dr. Tamara J. Moore is an associate professor of engineering education in the College of Engineering at Purdue University. Dr. Moore's research focuses on defining STEM integration through the use of engineering as the connection and investigating its power for student learning.

Dr. Jennifer Drake Patrick is an Assistant Professor of literacy education in the College of Education and Human Development. A former English/language arts teacher, Dr. Drake Patrick research is focused on disciplinary literacy.

Dr. Anthony Pellegrino is Assistant Professor of education in the College of Education and Human Development at George Mason University. A former social studies and history teacher, Anthony's research interests include youth-centered pedagogies and social science teacher preparation.

Dr. Susan Poland is a PhD student and Presidential Scholar at George Mason University focusing in science education research. With an undergraduate degree in integrated science education and a master's degree in curriculum and instruction focusing on STEM education, Susan has taught elementary, middle, and high school courses in engineering and all domains of science. Her research in the PhD program focuses on the enactment of scientific research in the classroom.

Dr. Bradley D. Rankin is a high school mathematics teacher at Wakefield High School in Arlington, Virginia. Bradley has been teaching mathematics for 20 years, is board certified, and has a Ph.D. in Mathematics Education Leadership from George Mason University.

Dr. Toni A. May is an Associate Professor of Assessment, Research, and Statistics in the School of Education at Drexel University. Dr. May's research is focused on assessment and evaluation in education with a focus on K-12 STEM.

Emily Bird is a high school Earth science teacher in Loudoun County Public Schools.

ACKNOWLEDGMENTS

This module was developed as a part of the STEM Road Map project (Carla C. Johnson, principal investigator). The Purdue University College of Education, General Motors, and other sources provided funding for this project.

See *www.routledge.com/9781138804234* for more information about *STEM Road Map: A Framework for Integrated STEM Education.*

PART 1

THE STEM ROAD MAP

BACKGROUND, THEORY, AND PRACTICE

OVERVIEW OF
THE *STEM ROAD MAP*
CURRICULUM SERIES

Carla C. Johnson, Erin E. Peters-Burton, and Tamara J. Moore

The *STEM Road Map Curriculum Series* was conceptualized and developed by a team of STEM educators from across the United States in response to a growing need to infuse real-world learning contexts, delivered through authentic problem-solving pedagogy, into K–12 classrooms. The curriculum series is grounded in integrated STEM, which focuses on the integration of the STEM disciplines – science, technology, engineering, and mathematics – delivered across content areas, incorporating the Framework for 21st Century Learning along with grade-level-appropriate academic standards. The curriculum series begins in kindergarten, with a five-week instructional sequence that introduces students to the STEM themes and gives them grade-level-appropriate topics and real-world challenges or problems to solve. The series uses project-based and problem-based learning, presenting students with the problem or challenge during the first lesson, and then teaching them science, social studies, English language arts, mathematics, and other content, as they apply what they learn to the challenge or problem at hand.

Authentic assessment and differentiation are embedded throughout the modules. Each *STEM Road Map Curriculum Series* module has a lead discipline, which may be science, social studies, English language arts, or mathematics. All disciplines are integrated into each module, along with ties to engineering. Another key component is the use of STEM Research Notebooks to allow students to track their own learning progress. The modules are designed with a scaffolded approach, with increasingly complex concepts and skills introduced as students' progress through grade levels.

The developers of this work view the curriculum as a resource that is intended to be used either as a whole or in part to meet the needs of districts, schools, and teachers who are implementing an integrated STEM approach. A variety of implementation formats are possible, from using one stand-alone module at a given grade level to using all five modules to provide 25 weeks of instruction. Also, within each grade band (K–2, 3–5, 6–8, 9–12), the modules can be sequenced in various ways to suit specific needs.

STANDARDS-BASED APPROACH

The *STEM Road Map Curriculum Series* is anchored in the *Next Generation Science Standards (NGSS)*, the *Common Core State Standards for Mathematics (CCSS Mathematics)*, the *Common Core State Standards for English Language Arts (CCSS ELA)*, and the Framework for 21st Century Learning. Each module includes a detailed curriculum map that incorporates the associated standards from the particular area correlated to lesson plans. The STEM Road Map has very clear and strong connections to these academic standards, and each of the grade-level topics was derived from the mapping of the standards to ensure alignment among topics, challenges or problems, and the required academic standards for students. Therefore, the curriculum series takes a standards-based approach and is designed to provide authentic contexts for application of required knowledge and skills.

THEMES IN THE *STEM ROAD MAP CURRICULUM SERIES*

The K–12 STEM Road Map is organized around five real-world STEM themes that were generated through an examination of the big ideas and challenges for society included in STEM standards and those that are persistent dilemmas for current and future generations:

- Cause and Effect

- Innovation and Progress

- The Represented World

- Sustainable Systems

- Optimizing the Human Experience

These themes are designed as springboards for launching students into an exploration of real-world learning situated within big ideas. Most important, the five STEM Road Map themes serve as a framework for scaffolding STEM learning across the K–12 continuum.

The themes are distributed across the STEM disciplines so that they represent the big ideas in science (Cause and Effect; Sustainable Systems), technology (Innovation and Progress; Optimizing the Human Experience), engineering (Innovation and Progress; Sustainable Systems; Optimizing the Human Experience), and mathematics (The Represented World), as well as concepts and challenges in social studies and 21st century skills that are also excellent contexts for learning in English language arts. The process of developing themes began with the clustering of the *NGSS* performance expectations and the National Academy of Engineering's grand challenges for engineering, which led to the development of the challenge in each module and connections of the module activities to the *CCSS Mathematics* and *CCSS ELA* standards. We performed these mapping processes with large teams of experts and found that these five themes provided breadth, depth, and coherence to frame a high-quality STEM learning experience from kindergarten through 12th grade.

Cause and Effect

The concept of cause and effect is a powerful and pervasive notion in the STEM fields. It is the foundation of understanding how and why things happen as they do. Humans spend considerable effort and resources trying to understand the causes and effects of natural and designed phenomena to gain better control over events and the environment and to be prepared to react appropriately. Equipped with the knowledge of a specific cause-and-effect relationship, we can lead better lives or contribute to the community by altering the cause, leading to a different effect. For example, if a person recognizes that irresponsible energy consumption leads to global climate change, that person can act to remedy his or her contribution to the situation. Although cause and effect is a core idea in the STEM fields, it can actually be difficult to determine. Students should be capable of understanding not only when evidence points to cause and effect but also when evidence points to relationships but not direct causality. The major goal of education is to foster students to be empowered, analytic thinkers, capable of thinking through complex processes to make important decisions. Understanding causality, as well as when it cannot be determined, will help students become better consumers, global citizens, and community members.

Innovation and Progress

One of the most important factors in determining whether humans will have a positive future is innovation. Innovation is the driving force behind progress, which helps create possibilities that did not exist before. Innovation and progress are creative entities, but in the STEM fields, they are anchored by evidence and logic, and they use established concepts to move the STEM fields forward. In creating something new, students must consider what is already known in the STEM fields and apply this knowledge appropriately. When we innovate, we create value that was not there previously and create new conditions and possibilities for even more innovations. Students should consider how their innovations might affect progress and use their STEM thinking to change current human burdens to benefits. For example, if we develop more efficient cars that use by-products from another manufacturing industry, such as food processing, then we have used waste productively and reduced the need for the waste to be hauled away, an indirect benefit of the innovation.

The Represented World

When we communicate about the world we live in, how the world works, and how we can meet the needs of humans, sometimes we can use the actual phenomena to

explain a concept. Sometimes, however, the concept is too big, too slow, too small, too fast, or too complex for us to explain using the actual phenomena, and we must use a representation or a model to help communicate the important features. We need representations and models such as graphs, tables, mathematical expressions, and diagrams because it makes our thinking visible. For example, when examining geologic time, we cannot actually observe the passage of such large chunks of time, so we create a timeline or a model that uses a proportional scale to visually illustrate how much time has passed for different eras. Another example may be something too complex for students at a particular grade level, such as explaining the *p* subshell orbitals of electrons to fifth graders. Instead, we use the Bohr model, which more closely represents the orbiting of planets and is accessible to fifth graders.

When we create models, they are helpful because they point out the most important features of a phenomenon. We also create representations of the world with mathematical functions, which help us change parameters to suit the situation. Creating representations of a phenomenon engages students because they are able to identify the important features of that phenomenon and communicate them directly. But because models are estimates of a phenomenon, they leave out some of the details, so it is important for students to evaluate their usefulness as well as their shortcomings.

Sustainable Systems

From an engineering perspective, the term *system* refers to the use of "concepts of component need, component interaction, systems interaction, and feedback. The interaction of subcomponents to produce a functional system is a common lens used by all engineering disciplines for understanding, analysis, and design." (Koehler, Bloom, and Binns 2013, p. 8). Systems can be either open (e.g., an ecosystem) or closed (e.g., a car battery). Ideally, a system should be sustainable, able to maintain equilibrium without much energy from outside the structure. Looking at a garden, we see flowers blooming, weeds sprouting, insects buzzing, and various forms of life living within its boundaries. This is an example of an ecosystem, a collection of living organisms that survive together, functioning as a system. The interaction of the organisms within the system and the influences of the environment (e.g., water, sunlight) can maintain the system for a period of time, thus demonstrating its ability to endure. Sustainability is a desirable feature of a system because it allows for existence of the entity in the long term.

In the STEM Road Map project, we identified different standards that we consider to be oriented toward systems that students should know and understand in the K–12 setting. These include ecosystems, the rock cycle, Earth processes (such as erosion, tectonics, ocean currents, weather phenomena), Earth-Sun-Moon cycles, heat transfer, and the interaction among the geosphere, biosphere, hydrosphere, and atmosphere. Students and teachers should understand that we live in a world of systems that are not independent of each other, but rather are intrinsically linked such that a disruption in one part of a system will have reverberating effects on other parts of the system.

Optimizing the Human Experience

Science, technology, engineering, and mathematics as disciplines have the capacity to continuously improve the ways humans live, interact, and find meaning in the world, thus working to optimize the human experience. This idea has two components: being more suited to our environment and being more fully human. For example, the progression of STEM ideas can help humans create solutions to complex problems, such as improving ways to access water sources, designing energy sources with minimal impact on our environment, developing new ways of communication and expression, and building efficient shelters. STEM ideas can also provide access to the secrets and wonders of nature. Learning in STEM requires students to think logically and systematically, which is a way of knowing the world that is markedly different from knowing the world as an artist. When students can employ various ways of knowing and understand when it is appropriate to use a different way of knowing or integrate ways of knowing, they are fully experiencing the best of what it is to be human. The problem-based learning scenarios provided in the STEM Road Map help students develop ways of thinking like STEM professionals as they ask questions and design solutions. They learn to optimize the human experience by innovating improvements in the designed world in which they live.

THE NEED FOR AN INTEGRATED STEM APPROACH

At a basic level, STEM stands for science, technology, engineering, and mathematics. Over the past decade, however, STEM has evolved to have a much broader scope and implications. Now, educators and policy makers refer to STEM as not only a concentrated area for investing in the future of the United States and other nations but also as a domain and mechanism for educational reform. The good intentions of the recent decade-plus of focus on accountability and increased testing has resulted in significant decreases not only in instructional time for teaching science and social studies but also in the flexibility of teachers to promote authentic, problem solving–focused classroom environments. The shift has had a detrimental impact on student acquisition of vitally important skills, which many refer to as 21st century skills, and often the ability of students to "think." Further, schooling has become increasingly siloed into compartments of mathematics, science, English language, arts and social studies, lacking any of the connections that are overwhelmingly present in the real world around children. Students have experienced school as content provided in boxes that must be memorized, devoid of any real-world context, and often have little understanding of why they are learning these things.

STEM-focused projects, curriculum, activities, and schools have emerged as a means to address these challenges. However, most of these efforts have continued to focus on the individual STEM disciplines (predominantly science and engineering) through more STEM classes and after-school programs in a "STEM enhanced" approach (Breiner et al. 2012). But in traditional and STEM enhanced approaches, there is little to no focus on other disciplines that are integral to the context of STEM in the real world. Integrated STEM education, on the other hand, infuses the learning of important STEM content and concepts with a much-needed emphasis on 21st century skills and a problem- and project-based pedagogy that more closely mirrors the real-world setting for society's challenges. It incorporates social studies, English language arts, and the arts as pivotal and necessary (Johnson 2013; Rennie, Venville, and Wallace 2012; Roehrig et al. 2012).

Framework for Stem Integration in The Classroom

The *STEM Road Map Curriculum Series* is grounded in the Framework for STEM Integration in the Classroom as conceptualized by Moore, Guzey, and Brown (2014) and Moore et al. (2014). The framework has six elements, described in the context of how they are used in the *STEM Road Map Curriculum Series* as follows:

1. The STEM Road Map contexts are meaningful to students and provide motivation to engage with the content. Together, these allow students to have different ways to enter into the challenge.

2. The STEM Road Map modules include engineering design that allows students to design technologies (i.e., products that are part of the designed world) for a compelling purpose.

3. The STEM Road Map modules provide students with the opportunities to learn from failure and redesign based on the lessons learned.

4. The STEM Road Map modules include standards-based disciplinary content as the learning objectives.

5. The STEM Road Map modules include student-centered pedagogies that allow students to grapple with the content, tie their ideas to the context, and learn to think for themselves as they deepen their conceptual knowledge.

6. The STEM Road Map modules emphasize 21st century skills and, in particular, highlight communication and teamwork.

All of the STEM Road Map modules incorporate these six elements; however, the level of emphasis on each of these elements varies based on the challenge or problem in each module.

THE NEED FOR THE *STEM ROAD MAP CURRICULUM SERIES*

As focus is increasing on integrated STEM, and additional schools and programs decide to move their curriculum and instruction in this direction, there is a need for high-quality, research-based curriculum designed with integrated STEM at the core. Several good resources are available to help teachers infuse engineering or more STEM enhanced approaches, but no curriculum exists that spans K–12 with an integrated STEM focus. The next chapter provides detailed information about the specific pedagogy, instructional strategies, and learning theory on which the *STEM Road Map Curriculum Series* is grounded.

REFERENCES

Breiner, J., M. Harkness, C. C. Johnson, and C. Koehler. 2012. What is STEM? A discussion about conceptions of STEM in education and partnerships. *School Science and Mathematics* 112 (1): 3–11.

Johnson, C. C. 2013. Conceptualizing integrated STEM education: Editorial. *School Science and Mathematics* 113 (8): 367–368.

Koehler, C. M., M. A. Bloom, and I. C. Binns. 2013. Lights, camera, action: Developing a methodology to document mainstream films' portrayal of nature of science and scientific inquiry. *Electronic Journal of Science Education* 17 (2).

Moore, T. J., S. S. Guzey, and A. Brown. 2014. Greenhouse design to increase habitable land: An engineering unit. *Science Scope* 51–57.

Moore, T. J., M. S. Stohlmann, H.-H. Wang, K. M. Tank, A. W. Glancy, and G. H. Roehrig. 2014. Implementation and integration of engineering in K–12 STEM education. In *Engineering in pre-college settings: Synthesizing research, policy, and practices,* ed. S. Purzer, J. Strobel, and M. Cardella, 35–60. West Lafayette, IN: Purdue Press.

Rennie, L., G. Venville, and J. Wallace. 2012. *Integrating science, technology, engineering, and mathematics: Issues, reflections, and ways forward.* New York: Routledge.

Roehrig, G. H., T. J. Moore, H. H. Wang, and M. S. Park. 2012. Is adding the *E* enough? Investigating the impact of K–12 engineering standards on the implementation of STEM integration. *School Science and Mathematics* 112 (1): 31–44.

STRATEGIES USED IN THE
STEM ROAD MAP
CURRICULUM SERIES

Erin E. Peters-Burton, Carla C. Johnson, Toni A. May, and Tamara J. Moore

The *STEM Road Map Curriculum Series* uses what has been identified through research as best-practice pedagogy, including embedded formative assessment strategies throughout each module. This chapter briefly describes the key strategies that are employed in the series.

PROJECT- AND PROBLEM-BASED LEARNING

Each module in the *STEM Road Map Curriculum Series* uses either project-based learning or problem-based learning to drive the instruction. Project-based learning begins with a driving question to guide student teams in addressing a contextualized local or com- munity problem or issue. The outcome of project-based instruction is a product that is conceptualized, designed, and tested through a series of scaffolded learning experiences (Blumenfeld et al. 1991; Krajcik and Blumenfeld 2006). Problem-based learning is often grounded in a fictitious scenario, challenge, or problem (Barell 2006; Lambros 2004). On the first day of instruction within the unit, student teams are provided with the context of the problem. Teams work through a series of activities and use open-ended research to develop their potential solution to the problem or challenge, which need not be a tangible product (Johnson 2003).

ENGINEERING DESIGN PROCESS

The *STEM Road Map Curriculum Series* uses engineering design as a way to facilitate integrated STEM within the modules. The engineering design process (EDP) is depicted in Figure 2.1 (p. 10). It highlights two major aspects of engineering design – problem scoping and solution generation – and six specific components of

DOI: 10.4324/9781003261766-3

Figure 2.1. Engineering Design Process

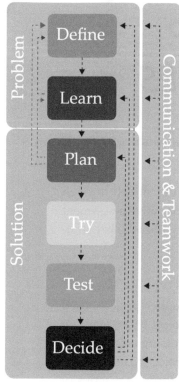

Engineering Design Process
A way to improve

Copyright © 2015 PictureSTEM-Purdue University Research Foundation

working toward a design: define the problem, learn about the problem, plan a solution, try the solution, test the solution, decide whether the solution is good enough. It also shows that communication and teamwork are involved throughout the entire process. As the arrows in the figure indicate, the order in which the components of engineering design are addressed depends on what becomes needed as designers progress through the EDP. Designers must communicate and work in teams throughout the process. The EDP is iterative, meaning that components of the process can be repeated as needed until the design is good enough to present to the client as a potential solution to the problem.

Problem scoping is the process of gathering and analyzing information to deeply understand the engineering design problem. It includes defining the problem and learning about the problem. Defining the problem includes identifying the problem, the client, and the end user of the design. The client is the person (or people) who hired the designers to do the work, and the end user is the person (or people) who will use the final design. The designers must also identify the criteria and the constraints of the problem. The criteria are the things the client wants from the solution, and the constraints are the things that limit the possible solutions. The designers must spend significant time learning about the problem, which can include activities such as the following:

- Reading informational texts and researching about relevant concepts or contexts

- Identifying and learning about needed mathematical and scientific skills, knowledge, and tools

- Learning about things done previously to solve similar problems

- Experimenting with possible materials that could be used in the design

Problem scoping also allows designers to consider how to measure the success of the design in addressing specific criteria and staying within the constraints over multiple iterations of solution generation.

Solution generation includes planning a solution, trying the solution, testing the solution, and deciding whether the solution is good enough. Planning the solution includes generating many design ideas that both address the criteria and meet the constraints.

Here the designers must consider what was learned about the problem during problem scoping. Design plans include clear communication of design ideas through media such as notebooks, blueprints, schematics, or storyboards. They also include details about the design, such as measurements, materials, colors, costs of materials, instructions for how things fit together, and sets of directions. Making the decision about which design idea to move forward involves considering the trade-offs of each design idea.

Once a clear design plan is in place, the designers must try the solution. Trying the solution includes developing a prototype (a testable model) based on the plan generated. The prototype might be something physical or a process to accomplish a goal. This com- ponent of design requires that the designers consider the risk involved in implementing the design. The prototype developed must be tested. Testing the solution includes con- ducting fair tests that verify whether the plan is a solution that is good enough to meet the client and end user needs and wants. Data need to be collected about the results of the tests of the prototype, and these data should be used to make evidence-based decisions regarding the design choices made in the plan. Here, the designers must again consider the criteria and constraints for the problem.

Using the data gathered from the testing, the designers must decide whether the solution is good enough to meet the client and end user needs and wants by assessment based on the criteria and constraints. Here, the designers must justify or reject design decisions based on the background research gathered while learning about the problem and on the evidence gathered during the testing of the solution. The designers must now decide whether to present the current solution to the client as a possibility or to do more iterations of design on the solution. If they decide that improvements need to be made to the solution, the designers must decide if there is more that needs to be understood about the problem, client, or end user; if another design idea should be tried; or if more planning needs to be conducted on the same design. One way or another, more work needs to be done.

Throughout the process of designing a solution to meet a client's needs and wants, designers work in teams and must communicate to each other, the client, and likely the end user. Teamwork is important in engineering design because multiple perspectives and differing skills and knowledge are valuable when working to solve problems. Communication is key to the success of the designed solution. Designers must communicate their ideas clearly using many different representations, such as text in an engineering notebook, diagrams, flowcharts, technical briefs, or memos to the client.

LEARNING CYCLE

The same format for the learning cycle is used in all grade levels throughout the STEM Road Map, so that students engage in a variety of activities to learn about phenomena in the modules thoroughly and have consistent experiences in the problem- and project- based learning modules. Expectations for learning by younger students are

not as high as for older students, but the format of the progression of learning is the same. Students who have learned with curriculum from the STEM Road Map in early grades know what to expect in later grades. The learning cycle consists of five parts – Introductory Activity/Engagement, Activity/Exploration, Explanation, Elaboration/ Application of Knowledge, and Evaluation/Assessment – and is based on the empirically tested 5E model from BSCS (Bybee et al. 2006).

In the Introductory Activity/Engagement phase, teachers introduce the module challenge and use a unique approach designed to pique students' curiosity. This phase gets students to start thinking about what they already know about the topic and begin wondering about key ideas. The Introductory Activity/Engagement phase positions students to be confident about what they are about to learn, because they have prior knowledge, and clues them into what they don't yet know.

In the Activity/Exploration phase, the teacher sets up activities in which students experience a deeper look at the topics that were introduced earlier. Students engage in the activities and generate new questions or consider possibilities using preliminary investigations. Students work independently, in small groups, and in whole-group settings to conduct investigations, resulting in common experiences about the topic and skills involved in the real-world activities. Teachers can assess students' development of concepts and skills based on the common experiences during this phase.

During the Explanation phase, teachers direct students' attention to concepts they need to understand and skills they need to possess to accomplish the challenge. Students participate in activities to demonstrate their knowledge and skills to this point, and teachers can pinpoint gaps in student knowledge during this phase.

In the Elaboration/Application of Knowledge phase, teachers present students with activities that engage in higher-order thinking to create depth and breadth of student knowledge, while connecting ideas across topics within and across STEM. Students apply what they have learned thus far in the module to a new context or elaborate on what they have learned about the topic to a deeper level of detail.

In the last phase, Evaluation/Assessment, teachers give students summative feedback on their knowledge and skills as demonstrated through the challenge. This is not the only point of assessment (as discussed in the section on Embedded Formative Assessments), but it is an assessment of the culmination of the knowledge and skills for the module. Students demonstrate their cognitive growth at this point and reflect on how far they have come since the beginning of the module. The challenges are designed to be multidimensional in the ways students must collaborate and communicate their new knowledge.

STEM RESEARCH NOTEBOOK

One of the main components of the *STEM Road Map Curriculum Series* is the STEM Research Notebook, a place for students to capture their ideas, questions, observations, reflections, evidence of progress, and other items associated with their daily work. At the beginning of each module, the teacher walks students through the setup of the STEM Research Notebook, which could be a three-ring binder, composition book, or spiral notebook. You may wish to have students create divided sections so that they can easily access work from various disciplines during the module. Electronic notebooks kept on student devices are also acceptable and encouraged. Students will develop their own table of contents and create chapters in the notebook for each module.

Each lesson in the *STEM Road Map Curriculum Series* includes one or more prompts that are designed for inclusion in the STEM Research Notebook and appear as questions or statements that the teacher assigns to students. These prompts require students to apply what they have learned across the lesson to solve the big problem or challenge for that module. Each lesson is designed to meaningfully refer students to the larger problem or challenge they have been assigned to solve with their teams. The STEM Research Notebook is designed to be a key formative assessment tool, as students' daily entries provide evidence of what they are learning. The notebook can be used as a mechanism for dialogue between the teacher and students, as well as for peer and self-evaluation.

The use of the STEM Research Notebook is designed to scaffold student notebooking skills across the grade bands in the *STEM Road Map Curriculum Series*. In the early grades, children learn how to organize their daily work in the notebook as a way to collect their products for future reference. In elementary school, students structure their notebooks to integrate background research along with their daily work and lesson prompts. In the upper grades (middle and high school), students expand their use of research and data gathering through team discussions to more closely mirror the work of STEM experts in the real world.

THE ROLE OF ASSESSMENT IN THE *STEM ROAD MAP CURRICULUM SERIES*

Starting in the middle years and continuing into secondary education, the word *assessment* typically brings grades to mind. These grades may take the form of a letter or a percentage, but they typically are used as a representation of a student's content mastery. If well thought out and implemented, however, classroom assessment can offer teachers, parents, and students valuable information about student learning and misconceptions that does not necessarily come in the form of a grade (Popham 2013).

The *STEM Road Map Curriculum Series* provides a set of assessments for each module. Teachers are encouraged to use assessment information for more than just assigning grades to students. Instead, assessments of activities requiring students to actively engage in their learning, such as student journaling in STEM Research Notebooks, collaborative presentations, and constructing graphic organizers, should be used to move student learning forward. Whereas other curriculum with assessments may include

objective-type (multiple-choice or matching) tests, quizzes, or worksheets, we have intentionally avoided these forms of assessments to better align assessment strategies with teacher instruction and student learning techniques. Since the focus of this book is on project- or problem-based STEM curriculum and instruction that focuses on higher-level thinking skills, appropriate and authentic performance assessments were developed to elicit the most reliable and valid indication of growth in student abilities (Brookhart and Nitko 2008).

Comprehensive Assessment System

Assessment throughout all STEM Road Map curriculum modules acts as a comprehensive system in which formative and summative assessments work together to pro- vide teachers with high-quality information on student learning. Formative assessment occurs when the teacher finds out formally or informally what a student knows about a smaller, defined concept or skill and provides timely feedback to the student about his or her level of proficiency. Summative assessments occur when students have performed all activities in the module and are given a cumulative performance evaluation in which they demonstrate their growth in learning.

A comprehensive assessment system can be thought of as akin to a sporting event. Formative assessments are the practices: It is important to accomplish them consistently, they provide feedback to help students improve their learning, and making mistakes can be worthwhile if students are given an opportunity to learn from them. Summative assessments are the competitions: Students need to be prepared to perform at the best of their ability. Without multiple opportunities to practice skills along the way through formative assessments, students will not have the best chance of demonstrating growth in abilities through summative assessments (Black and Wiliam 1998).

Embedded Formative Assessments

Formative assessments in this module serve two main purposes: to provide feedback to students about their learning and to provide important information for the teacher to inform immediate instructional needs. Providing feedback to students is particularly important when conducting problem- or project-based learning because students take on much of the responsibility for learning, and teachers must facilitate student learning in an informed way. For example, if students are required to conduct research for the Activity/Exploration phase but are not familiar with what constitutes a reliable resource, they may develop misconceptions based on poor information. When a teacher monitors this learning through formative assessments and provides specific feedback related to the instructional goals, students are less likely to develop incomplete or incorrect conceptions in their independent investigations. By using formative assessment to detect problems in student learning and then acting on this information, teachers help move student learning forward through these teachable moments.

Formative assessments come in a variety of formats. They can be informal, such as asking students probing questions related to student knowledge or tasks or simply observing students engaged in an activity to gather information about student skills. Formative assessments can also be formal, such as a written quiz or a laboratory practical.

Regardless of the type, three key steps must be completed when using formative assessments (Sondergeld, Bell, and Leusner 2010). First, the assessment is delivered to students so that teachers can collect data. Next, teachers analyze the data (student responses) to determine student strengths and areas that need additional support. Finally, teachers use the results from information collected to modify lessons and create learning environments that reinforce weak points in student learning. If student learning information is not used to modify instruction, the assessment cannot be considered formative in nature. Formative assessments can be about content, science process skills, or even learning skills. When a formative assessment focuses on content, it assesses student knowledge about the disciplinary core ideas from the *Next Generation Science Standards* (*NGSS*) or content objectives from *Common Core State Standards for Mathematics* (*CCSS Mathematics*) or *Common Core State Standards for English Language Arts* (*CCSS ELA*). Content-focused formative assessments ask students questions about declarative knowledge regarding the concepts they have been learning. Process skills formative assessments examine the extent to which a student can perform science and engineering practices from the *NGSS* or process objectives from *CCSS Mathematics* or *CCSS ELA*, such as constructing an argument. Learning skills can also be assessed formatively by asking students to reflect on the ways they learn best during a module and identify ways they could have learned more.

Assessment Maps

Assessment maps or blueprints can be used to ensure alignment between classroom instruction and assessment. If what students are learning in the classroom is not the same as the content on which they are assessed, the resultant judgment made on student learning will be invalid (Brookhart and Nitko 2008). Therefore, the issue of instruction and assessment alignment is critical. The assessment map for this book (found in Chapter 3) indicates by lesson whether the assessment should be completed as a group or on an individual basis, identifies the assessment as formative or summative in nature, and aligns the assessment with its corresponding learning objectives.

Note that the module includes far more formative assessments than summative assessments. This is done intentionally to provide students with multiple opportunities to practice their learning of new skills before completing a summative assessment. Note also that formative assessments are used to collect information on only one or two learning objectives at a time so that potential relearning or instructional modifications can focus on smaller and more manageable chunks of information. Conversely,

summative assessments in the module cover many more learning objectives, as they are traditionally used as final markers of student learning. This is not to say that information collected from summative assessments cannot or should not be used formatively. If teachers find that gaps in student learning persist after a summative assessment is completed, it is important to revisit these existing misconceptions or areas of weakness before moving on (Black et al. 2003).

SELF-REGULATED LEARNING THEORY IN THE STEM ROAD MAP MODULES

Many learning theories are compatible with the STEM Road Map modules, such as constructivism, situated cognition, and meaningful learning. However, we feel that the self-regulated learning theory (SRL) aligns most appropriately (Zimmerman 2000). SRL requires students to understand that thinking needs to be motivated and managed (Ritchhart, Church, and Morrison 2011). The STEM Road Map modules are student centered and are designed to provide students with choices, concrete hands-on experiences, and opportunities to see and make connections, especially across subjects (Eliason and Jenkins 2012; NAEYC 2016). Additionally, SRL is compatible with the modules because it fosters a learning environment that supports students' motivation, enables students to become aware of their own learning strategies, and requires reflection on learning while experiencing the module (Peters and Kitsantas 2010).

The theory behind SRL (see Figure 2.2) explains the different processes that students engage in before, during, and after a learning task. Because SRL is a cyclical learning process, the accomplishment of one cycle develops strategies for the next learning cycle. This cyclic way of learning aligns with the various sections in the STEM Road Map lesson plans on Introductory Activity/ Engagement, Activity/ Exploration, Explanation, Elaboration/Application of Knowledge, and Evaluation/Assessment. Since the students engaged in a module take on much of the responsibility for learning, this theory also provides guidance for teachers to keep students on the right track.

Figure 2.2. SRL Theory

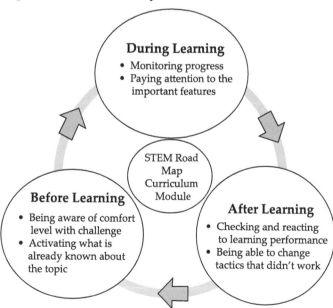

Source: Adapted from Zimmerman (2000).

Table 2.1. SRL Learning Process Components

Learning Process Components	Example from Rebuilding the Natural Environment Module	Lesson Number
Before Learning		
Motivates students	Students brainstorm their own experiences with energy consumption.	Lesson 1
Evokes prior learning	Students will discuss their understanding of electricity generation within teams and share their ideas with the class. Students will be asked to give their responses on the following questions: (a) What is electricity? (b) How is it generated? (c) How does it get to our houses?	Lesson 1
During Learning		
Focuses on important features	Students must determine the cost-effectiveness of taking a single-family home off the current electrical grid and powering it solely from available renewable/sustainable energy sources. Students will need to research the energy output of devices, use weather data to accurately estimate the amount of time each device will be able to generate electricity (amount of sunlight per day and season for solar, average amount of wind per day and season for wind, etc.), and conservatively calculate the kilowatt hours generated on average for a whole-home system.	Lesson 3
Helps students monitor their progress	Teacher monitors student STEM Research Notebooks for the accuracy of each device and for how the devices work as a system.	Lesson 3
After Learning		
Evaluates learning	Students receive feedback on the rubric for their innovation for their group work and for their individual work.	Lesson 4
Takes account of what worked and what did not work	Students will write a reflection on the quality of their work given feedback from the class and teacher.	Lesson 4

The remainder of this section explains how SRL theory is embedded within the five sections of each module and points out ways to support students in becoming independent learners of STEM while productively functioning in collaborative teams.

Before Learning: Setting the Stage

Before attempting a learning task such as the STEM Road Map modules, teachers should develop an understanding of their students' level of comfort with the process of accomplishing the learning and determine what they already know about the topic. When students are comfortable with attempting a learning task, they tend to take more risks in learning and as a result achieve deeper learning (Bandura 1986).

The STEM Road Map curriculum modules are designed to foster excitement from the very beginning. Each module has an Introductory Activity/Engagement section that introduces the overall topic from a unique and exciting perspective, engaging the students to learn more so that they can accomplish the challenge. The Introductory Activity also has a design component that helps teachers assess what students already know about the topic of the module. In addition to the deliberate designs in the lesson plans to support SRL, teachers can support a high level of student comfort with the learning challenge by finding out if students have ever accomplished the same kind of task and, if so, asking them to share what worked well for them.

During Learning: Staying the Course

Some students fear inquiry learning because they aren't sure what to do to be successful (Peters 2010). However, the STEM Road Map curriculum modules are embedded with tools to help students pay attention to knowledge and skills that are important for the learning task and to check student understanding along the way. One of the most important processes for learning is the ability for learners to monitor their own progress while performing a learning task (Peters 2012). The modules allow students to monitor their progress with tools such as the STEM Research Notebooks, in which they record what they know and can check whether they have acquired a complete set of knowledge and skills. The STEM Road Map modules support inquiry strategies that include previewing, questioning, predicting, clarifying, observing, discussing, and journaling (Morrison and Milner 2014). Through the use of technology throughout the modules, inquiry is supported by providing students access to resources and data while enabling them to process information, report the findings, collaborate, and develop 21st century skills.

It is important for teachers to encourage students to have an open mind about alternative solutions and procedures (Milner and Sondergeld 2015) when working through the STEM Road Map curriculum modules. Novice learners can have difficulty knowing what to pay attention to and tend to treat each possible avenue for information as equal (Benner 1984). Teachers are the mentors in a classroom and can point out ways for students to approach learning during the Activity/Exploration, Explanation, and Elaboration/Application of Knowledge portions of the lesson plans to ensure that students pay attention to the important concepts and skills throughout the module. For example, if a student is to demonstrate conceptual awareness of motion when working on roller coaster research, but the student has misconceptions about motion, the teacher can step in and redirect student learning.

After Learning: Knowing What Works

The classroom is a busy place, and it may often seem that there is no time for self-reflection on learning. Although skipping this reflective process may save time in the short term, it reduces the ability to take into account things that worked well and things that didn't so that teaching the module may be improved next time. In the long run, SRL skills are critical for students to become independent learners who can adapt to new situations. By investing the time it takes to teach students SRL skills, teachers can save time later, because students will be able to apply methods and approaches for learning that they have found effective to new situations. In the Evaluation/Assessment portion of the STEM Road Map curriculum modules, as well as in the formative assessments throughout the modules, two processes in the after-learning phase are supported: evaluating one's own performance and accounting for ways to adapt tactics that didn't work well. Students have many opportunities to self-assess in formative assessments, both in groups and individually, using the rubrics provided in the modules.

The designs of the *NGSS* and *CCSS* allow for students to learn in diverse ways, and the STEM Road Map curriculum modules emphasize that students can use a variety of tactics to complete the learning process. For example, students can use STEM Research Notebooks to record what they have learned during the various research activities. Note-book entries might include putting objectives in students' own words, compiling their prior learning on the topic, documenting new learning, providing proof of what they learned, and reflecting on what they felt successful doing and what they felt they still needed to work on. Perhaps students didn't realize that they were supposed to connect what they already knew with what they learned. They could record this and would be prepared in the next learning task to begin connecting prior learning with new learning.

SAFETY IN STEM

Student safety is a primary consideration in all subjects but is an area of particular concern in science, where students may interact with unfamiliar tools and materials that may pose additional safety risks. It is important to implement safety practices within the context of STEM investigations, whether in a classroom laboratory or in the field.

When you keep safety in mind as a teacher, you avoid many potential issues with the lesson while also protecting your students.

STEM safety practices encompass things considered in the typical science classroom. Ensure that students are familiar with basic safety considerations, such as wearing protective equipment (e.g., safety glasses or goggles and latex-free gloves) and taking care with sharp objects, and know emergency exit procedures. Teachers should learn beforehand the locations of the safety eyewash, fume hood, fire extinguishers, and emergency shut-off switch in the classroom and how to use them. Also be aware of any school or district safety policies that are in place and apply those that align with the work being conducted in the lesson. It is important to review all safety procedures annually.

STEM investigations should always be supervised. Each lesson in the modules includes teacher guidelines for applicable safety procedures that should be followed. Before each investigation, teachers should go over these safety procedures with the student teams. Some STEM focus areas such as engineering require that students can demonstrate how to properly use equipment in the maker space before the teacher allows them to proceed with the lesson.

Information about classroom science safety, including a safety checklist for science class- rooms, general lab safety recommendations, and links to other science safety resources, is available at the Council of State Science Supervisors (CSSS) website at *www.csss-science. org/safety.shtml*. The National Science Teaching Association (NSTA) provides a list of science rules and regulations, including standard operating procedures for lab safety, and a safety acknowledgment form for students and parents or guardians to sign. You can access these resources at *http://static.nsta.org/pdfs/SafetyIn TheScienceClassroom.pdf*. In addition, NSTA's Safety in the Science Classroom web page (*www.nsta.org/safety*) has numerous links to safety resources, including papers written by the NSTA Safety Advisory Board.

Disclaimer: The safety precautions for each activity are based on use of the recommended materials and instructions, legal safety standards, and better professional practices. Using alternative materials or procedures for these activities may jeopardize the level of safety and therefore is at the user's own risk.

REFERENCES

Bandura, A. 1986. *Social foundations of thought and action: A social cognitive theory*. Englewood Cliffs, NJ: Prentice-Hall.

Barell, J. 2006. *Problem-based learning: An inquiry approach*. Thousand Oaks, CA: Corwin Press.

Benner, P. 1984. *From novice to expert: Excellence and power in clinical nursing practice*. Menlo Park, CA: Addison-Wesley Publishing Company.

Black, P., C. Harrison, C. Lee, B. Marshall, and D. Wiliam. 2003. *Assessment for learning: Putting it into practice*. Berkshire, UK: Open University Press.

Black, P., and D. Wiliam. 1998. Inside the black box: Raising standards through classroom assessment. *Phi Delta Kappan* 80 (2): 139–148.

Blumenfeld, P., E. Soloway, R. Marx, J. Krajcik, M. Guzdial, and A. Palincsar. 1991. Motivating project- based learning: Sustaining the doing, supporting learning. *Educational Psychologist* 26 (3): 369–398.

Brookhart, S. M., and A. J. Nitko. 2008. *Assessment and grading in classrooms.* Upper Saddle River, NJ: Pearson.

Bybee, R., J. Taylor, A. Gardner, P. Van Scotter, J. Carlson, A. Westbrook, and N. Landes. 2006. *The BSCS 5E instructional model: Origins and effectiveness. http://science.education.nih.gov/ houseofreps. nsf/b82d55fa138783c2852572c9004f5566/$FILE/Appendix?D.pdf.*

Eliason, C. F., and L. T. Jenkins. 2012. *A practical guide to early childhood curriculum.* 9th ed. New York: Merrill.

Johnson, C. 2003. Bioterrorism is real-world science: Inquiry-based simulation mirrors real life. *Science Scope* 27 (3): 19–23.

Krajcik, J., and P. Blumenfeld. 2006. Project-based learning. In *The Cambridge handbook of the learning sciences,* ed. R. Keith Sawyer, 317–334. New York: Cambridge University Press.

Lambros, A. 2004. *Problem-based learning in middle and high school classrooms: A teacher's guide to implementation.* Thousand Oaks, CA: Corwin Press.

Milner, A. R., and T. Sondergeld. 2015. Gifted urban middle school students: The inquiry continuum and the nature of science. *National Journal of Urban Education and Practice* 8 (3): 442–461.

Morrison, V., and A. R. Milner. 2014. Literacy in support of science: A closer look at cross- curricular instructional practice. *Michigan Reading Journal* 46 (2): 42–56.

National Association for the Education of Young Children (NAEYC). 2016. Developmentally appropriate practice position statements. *www.naeyc.org/positionstatements/dap.*

Peters, E. E. 2010. Shifting to a student-centered science classroom: An exploration of teacher and student changes in perceptions and practices. *Journal of Science Teacher Education* 21 (3): 329–349.

Peters, E. E. 2012. Developing content knowledge in students through explicit teaching of the nature of science: Influences of goal setting and self- monitoring. *Science and Education* 21 (6): 881–898.

Peters, E. E., and A. Kitsantas. 2010. The effect of nature of science metacognitive prompts on science students' content and nature of science knowledge, metacognition, and self- regulatory efficacy. *School Science and Mathematics* 110: 382–396.

Popham, W. J. 2013. *Classroom assessment: What teachers need to know.* 7th ed. Upper Saddle River, NJ: Pearson.

Ritchhart, R., M. Church, and K. Morrison. 2011. *Making thinking visible: How to promote engagement, understanding, and independence for all learners.* San Francisco, CA: Jossey-Bass.

Sondergeld, T. A., C. A. Bell, and D. M. Leusner. 2010. Understanding how teachers engage in formative assessment. *Teaching and Learning* 24 (2): 72–86.

Zimmerman, B. J. 2000. Attaining self-regulation: A social-cognitive perspective. In *Handbook of self-regulation,* ed. M. Boekaerts, P. Pintrich, and M. Zeidner, 13–39. San Diego: Academic Press.

PART 2

FORMATION OF THE EARTH

STEM ROAD MAP MODULE

MODULE OVERVIEW – FORMATION OF THE EARTH

Anthony Pellegrino, Emily Bird, Erin E. Peters-Burton, Jennifer Drake Patrick, Bradley D. Rankin, Susan Poland, Janet B. Walton, and Carla C. Johnson

THEME: Cause and Effect

LEAD DISCIPLINES: Science

MODULE SUMMARY

By ninth grade, students have formed nascent ideas about the early history of the Earth, but likely have not yet connected theories about the formation of the Earth to processes taking place since the proliferation of humans. In this module, students will explore the periods, eras, and epochs that have unfolded over Earth's history to determine indices and boundaries that help scientists describe large time periods. Students will research how geologists and other Earth science professionals gather information about very old and very slow phenomena in order to formulate and support their claims about the connections between early and current processes we observe on Earth (Peters-Burton, Seshaiyer, Burton, Drake-Patrick, and Johnson, 2015, p. 127; see https://www.routledge.com/products/9781138804234).

Students will apply that work to identify, define and describe attributes scientists use in these pursuits to delineate Earth's eras, periods, and epochs to ultimately determine the appropriate boundary event to define the Anthropocene Epoch, a designation about which there is significant scientific debate. Although human impact on Earth's formation processes is generally accepted in the scientific community, the identification of a distinct Anthropocene Epoch in which human activities have significantly impacted the earth, continues to be debated. Likewise, boundaries for this epoch are also less clear. To that end students will weigh into this debate and work to discern whether, for example, the origination of agriculture, the Age of European exploration, the Industrial Revolution, the Great Acceleration, or the Information Age mark the beginning of this time. Such deliberation offers clear connections to science standards and those of other disciplines, including mathematics, English language arts, and social studies. The lessons learned from this PBL module will include helping students

DOI: 10.4324/9781003261766-5

recognize the tools, ideas, and theories scientists use and consider when determining boundaries and transitions of Earth's geological periods. Likewise, students will apply that understanding to our current time, the Anthropocene Epoch, to better understand humanity's impact on the planet.

Two motivational components are built into this project: connecting to prior knowledge, and designing a multimedia project and publication-ready textbook entry for a textbook company, helping to determine whether and how to portray the Anthropocene Epoch in a new edition of an Earth science textbook. Students will also utilize technology to communicate this information effectively through a variety of media (adapted from Peters-Burton et al., 2015; see https://www.routledge.com/products/9781138804234).

ESTABLISHED GOALS/OBJECTIVES

The goal for this PBL module is for students to create a multimedia presentation and textbook entry that uses geologic theory and standards of measurement to determine the boundary for the Anthropocene. Students will gather data on past eras, periods, and epochs and apply the methods in which geologists and other scientists use to determine boundary dates and events. This presentation will be developed to assist a textbook publishing company in presenting the Anthropocene Epoch in a new edition of an Earth science textbook for high school students.

At the conclusion of this module students will be able to:

a. Identify, define, and describe attributes of eras, periods, and epochs which have marked geologic time in Earth's history

b. Evaluate various possible index layers and boundary events that mark the beginning of the Anthropocene Epoch to determine which is most appropriate when labeling the current epoch in Earth's history

c. Design and present a multimedia presentation to share with textbook publishers regarding information on the Anthropocene Epoch to include in a secondary-level Earth science textbook

d. Create a publication-ready textbook entry describing the Anthropocene Epoch

The themes in the project include:

• Examination of the social impact of humans on the planet and how humans have affected processes involved in Earth's evolution

• The discernable changes to weather, climate, ocean and air composition from energy consumption, population growth, migration and development patterns

Discipline-specific objectives include:

- Social studies objectives include applying principles of historical thinking including perspective and interpretation of evidence to determine boundary events that characterize the Anthropocene Epoch

- English language arts objectives include engaging in argument from evidence, obtaining, evaluating, and communicating information related to geologic phenomena.

- Mathematics objectives include utilizing mathematical reasoning and calculation skills to support scientific research into boundary events that characterize geologic periods, eras, and epochs

- Science and engineering objectives include developing and using models, planning and carrying out investigations, analyzing and interpreting data, using mathematics and computational thinking, constructing explanations (for science) and designing solutions (for engineering).

CHALLENGE AND/OR PROBLEM FOR STUDENTS TO SOLVE
The Era of Humans (Anthropocene) Challenge

Students are challenged to gather data related to geologic time scales and apply them to potential boundary events that are best suited to mark the beginning of the Anthropocene Epoch. From this examination, students will present their recommendations to textbook publishers interested in whether and how to include information on this epoch in Earth science textbooks. As such, student groups will be tasked with persuading publishers then writing a textbook entry (including various forms of media) suitable for the intended audience.

Driving questions for this unit include:

- How have geologists characterized various periods, eras, and epochs when developing ideas about the Earth's formation?

- How has the proliferation of humans on Earth fundamentally affected the planet's formation processes?

- What are the specific boundary events that have characterized the current period in Earth's formation?

- Why do humans feel the need to assign boundaries and names for periods of time?

STEM RESEARCH NOTEBOOK

Each student will maintain a STEM Research Notebook that will serve as a place for students to organize their work throughout the module. All written work in the module should be included in the notebook including records of students' thoughts and ideas, fictional accounts based on the concepts in the module, and records of student progress through the EDP. The notebooks may be maintained across subject areas, giving students the opportunity to see that although their classes may be separated during the school day the knowledge they gain is connected.

A three-ring binder works well for the Research Notebooks since students will include a variety of handouts in the Research Notebook. You may wish to have students create divided sections in order to easily access work from various disciplines during the module. Students will have the opportunity to create a cover and table of contents for their Research Notebooks (see Lesson 1 Activity/Investigation, ELA). You may also wish to have students include the STEM Research Notebook Guidelines provided below in their notebooks.

Emphasize to students that scientists and other researchers maintain detailed Research Notebooks in their work. These notebooks are crucial to researchers' work since they contain critical information and track the researchers' progress. These notebooks are often considered legal documents for scientists who are pursuing patents or who wish to provide proof of their discovery process. Introduce to students the importance of organizing all information in a Research Notebook.

STUDENT HANDOUT

STEM RESEARCH NOTEBOOK GUIDELINES

STEM professionals record their ideas, inventions, experiments, questions, observations, and other work details in notebooks so that they can use these notebooks to help them think about their projects and the problems they are trying to solve. You will each keep a STEM Research Notebook during this module that is like the notebooks that STEM professionals use. In this notebook, you will include all your work and notes about ideas you have. The notebook will help you connect your daily work with the big problem or challenge you are working to solve.

It is important that you organize your notebook entries under the following headings:

1. **Chapter Topic or Title of Problem or Challenge:** You will start a new chapter in your STEM Research Notebook for each new module. This heading is the topic or title of the big problem or challenge that your team is working to solve in this module.

2. **Date and Topic of Lesson Activity for the Day:** Each day, you will begin your daily entry by writing the date and the day's lesson topic at the top of a new page. Write the page number both on the page and in the table of contents.

3. **Information Gathered From Research:** This is information you find from outside resources such as websites or books.

4. **Information Gained From Class or Discussions With Team Members:** This information includes any notes you take in class and notes about things your team discusses. You can include drawings of your ideas here, too.

5. **New Data Collected From Investigations:** This includes data gathered from experiments, investigations, and activities in class.

6. **Documents:** These are handouts and other resources you may receive in class that will help you solve your big problem or challenge. Paste or staple these documents in your STEM Research Notebook for safekeeping and easy access later.

7. **Personal Reflections:** Here, you record your own thoughts and ideas on what you are learning.

8. **Lesson Prompts:** These are questions or statements that your teacher assigns you within each lesson to help you solve your big problem or challenge. You will respond to the prompts in your notebook.

9. **Other Items:** This section includes any other items your teacher gives you or other ideas or questions you may have.

MODULE LAUNCH

In the opening activity, students will use Google Earth or other similar satellite sites to explore several features of the planet that are present as a result of formation processes. Specifically, students will focus on landforms that are the result of plate tectonics, such as the puzzle-piece shapes of the continents, mountain ranges, or actively rifting areas like the Mid-Atlantic Ridge or the Red Sea. Students may write about/speculate how those came about and how long those processes took.

PREREQUISITE KEY KNOWLEDGE

It is likely that the students engaging in this module have had some experience with Earth science in elementary and middle school, so they should have some knowledge about the basic principles of Earth as a planet in our solar system, its general physical properties, and scientific phenomena that guide its evolution. Foundational knowledge around these ideas will be important for successful implementation of the project. Ideally students will also have some working knowledge of technology and ways to create using technology. This might include intermediate knowledge of websites such as Google Earth, presentation software such as Prezi or PowerPoint, and shared file management platforms such as Google Docs.

Table 3.1. Prerequisite Key Knowledge and Sample Differentiation Strategies

Prerequisite key knowledge	Application of knowledge	Differentiation for students needing additional support
Dynamic nature of the Earth	Students will investigate how scientists have come to classify various time periods in the history of the Earth by looking to threshold and boundary events that characterize each period, era, or epoch.	Students needing support to better understand the dynamic nature of the Earth can view the introductory video from the Big History curriculum which offers a clear and visually compelling presentation of the formation of the Earth and the role of humans in our world. https://www.bighistoryproject.com/home
Evolution of life	Students will use their knowledge of phenomena related to evolution to discern how scientists have come to see various time periods in Earth's formation.	This brief (4 minute) video is designed to introduce middle and high school students to evolution through powerful images. See https://www.youtube.com/watch?v=FpfAZaVhx3k

Table 3.1. (*continued*)

Prerequisite key knowledge	Application of knowledge	Differentiation for students needing additional support
Human impact on the environment	Students will be looking across data related to climate changes and energy use to discern patterns related to human impact on the environment.	The series of images, text, and interactive features from National Geographic offers some powerful and informative visuals of humanity's impact on the environment. http://www.nationalgeographic.com/earthpulse/human-impact.html
Interpret scientific evidence	Students will review geologic and other scientific data.	The following video offers some introductory information regarding how and why scientists use and interpret data. This video might also be useful for teachers as the narrator provides recommendations on data collection and interpretation tools for students. https://www.youtube.com/watch?v=9NkT-oYPkOA
Interpret historical evidence	Students will look to potential boundary events and determine which is best suited to be presented as the boundary for the Anthropocene Epoch.	The Stanford History Education Group offers a comprehensive website dedicated to supporting students' historical thinking. It includes basic information about how to use historical evidence to make informed interpretations about the past. This site may be particularly useful for teachers who embark on this PBL unit without the support of history colleagues and students. https://sheg.stanford.edu/

POTENTIAL STEM MISCONCEPTIONS

Students enter the classroom with a wide variety of prior knowledge and ideas, so it is important to be alert to misconceptions, or inappropriate understandings of foundational knowledge. These misconceptions can be classified as one of several types: "preconceived notions," opinions based on popular beliefs or understandings; "nonscientific beliefs," knowledge students have gained about science from sources outside the scientific community; "conceptual misunderstandings," incorrect conceptual models based on incomplete understanding of concepts; "vernacular misconceptions," misunderstandings of words based on their common use versus their scientific use; and "factual misconceptions," incorrect or imprecise knowledge learned in early life that remains unchallenged (NRC 1997, p. 28). Misconceptions must be addressed and

dismantled in order for students to reconstruct their knowledge, and therefore teachers should be prepared to take the following steps:

- *Identify students' misconceptions.*

- *Provide a forum for students to confront their misconceptions.*

- *Help students reconstruct and internalize their knowledge, based on scientific models.* *(NRC 1997, p. 29)*

Keeley and Harrington (2010) recommend using diagnostic tools such as probes and formative assessment to identify and confront student misconceptions and begin the process of reconstructing student knowledge. Keeley and Harrington's *Uncovering Student Ideas in Science* series contains probes targeted toward uncovering student misconceptions in a variety of areas.

Some commonly held misconceptions specific to lesson content are provided with each lesson so that you can be alert for student misunderstanding of the science concepts presented and used during this module. The American Association for the Advancement of Science has also identified misconceptions that students frequently hold regarding various science concepts (see the links at *http://assessment.aaas.org/topics*).

Table 3.2. Sample STEM Misconceptions

Topic	Student Misconception	Explanation
Engineering Design Process (EDP)	Engineers use only the scientific process to solve problems in their work.	The scientific method is used to test predictions and explanations about the world. The EDP, on the other hand, is used to create a solution to a problem. In reality, engineers use both processes (see Teacher Background section in Lesson 2 for more information about the differences and similarities between the scientific method and the EDP).
Eras of the Earth or the Geological Column	There is one 'geological column' for the whole Earth.	The geological timescale divides the 4.5 billion years of earth history into distinct chunks, based on changes in environment or dominant forms of life over time. However, this does not mean that every rock of a particular age is the same. Just like today, in these periods many different processes were leaving their own unique record; marine deposits formed in shallow seas, deltas built out from coastlines, deserts formed vast dune fields. In other places, uplift of ancient mountain ranges led to no deposition, and erosion of rocks that had been laid down in earlier times. So there is no one geological column; each area has its own unique sequence of rock types, often with large time gaps in between different units. Correlating them all with each other is one of the major tasks of the geologist.
	Geologists can tell the age of a rock just from one small sample.	The most interesting geological information often comes from features which are only found at larger scales than a pebble – where a particular rock type occurs in a sequence, for example, or the sedimentary structures or deformation that are found in large outcrops.

SAMPLE STRATEGIES FOR DIFFERENTIATING INSTRUCTION WITHIN THIS MODULE

For the purposes of this curriculum module, differentiated instruction is conceptualized as a way to tailor instruction (including process, content, and product) to various student needs in your class. A number of differentiation strategies are integrated into lessons across the module. The problem and/or project based learning (PBL) approach used in the lessons is designed to address students' multiple intelligences by providing a variety of entry points and methods to investigate the key concepts in the module (for example, investigating the development of tall tower technologies throughout history). Differentiation strategies for students needing support in prerequisite knowledge can be found in the Prerequisite Key Knowledge section. You are encouraged to use information gained about student prior knowledge during introductory activities and discussions to inform your instructional differentiation. Strategies incorporated into this lesson include:

Flexible Grouping: Students work collaboratively in a variety of activities throughout this module. Grouping strategies you may choose to employ include student-led grouping, placing students in groups according to ability level, grouping students randomly, or grouping them so that students in each group have complementary strengths (for instance, one student might be strong in mathematics, another in art, and another in writing). You may also wish to use information about student prior knowledge about metabolism and cellular respiration for grouping purposes. Beginning in Lesson 2, you may wish to maintain the student groupings from Lesson 1 or regroup students according to one of the strategies described here. You may therefore wish to consider grouping students in Lesson 2 into design teams that they will maintain throughout the remainder of the module.

Various Environmental Learning Contexts: Students have the opportunity to learn in various contexts throughout the module, including alone, in groups, in quiet reading and research-oriented activities, and in active learning in inquiry and design activities. In addition, students learn in a variety of ways including inquiry activities, journaling, reading fiction and non-fiction texts, watching videos, class discussion, and conducting web-based research.

Assessments: Students are assessed in a variety of ways throughout the module, including individual and collaborative formative and summative assessments. Students have the opportunity to produce work via written text, oral presentations, media presentation, and modeling. You may choose to provide students with additional choices of media for their products (for example PowerPoint presentations, posters, or student-created websites or blogs).

Other strategies you may choose to employ include:

Compacting: Based upon student prior knowledge you may wish to adjust instructional activities for students who exhibit prior mastery of a learning objective. For

instance, if some students exhibit mastery of cellular respiration in Lesson 1, you may wish to limit the amount of time they spend practicing these skills and instead introduce ELA or social studies connections with associated activities.

Tiered Assignments and Scaffolding: Based upon your understanding of student ability, you may wish to provide students with variations on activities by adding complexity to assignments and/or providing more or fewer learning supports for activities throughout the module based upon student understanding of concepts and mastery of skills. For instance, some students may need additional support in identifying key search words and phrases for web-based research or may benefit from cloze sentence handouts to enhance vocabulary understanding. Other students may benefit from expanded reading selections and additional reflective writing. Others may benefit from working with manipulatives and other visual representations of mathematical concepts. You may also wish to work with your school librarian to compile a set of topical resources at a variety of reading levels.

Strategies for English Language Learners (ELLs): Students who are developing proficiency in English language skills require additional supports to simultaneously learn academic content and the specialized language associated with specific content areas. WIDA has created a framework for providing support to these students and provides rubrics and guidance on differentiating instructional materials for ELLs, providing five overarching learning standards (see https://www.wida.us/get.aspx?id=7). In particular, ELL students may benefit from additional sensory supports including images, physical modeling, and graphic representations of module content as well as interactive support through collaborative work. This module incorporates a variety of sensory supports and provides ongoing opportunities for ELL students to work with collaboratively. The focus in this module on geologic processes and the impact of human activity on the climate and ecosystems provides opportunities to access the culturally diverse experiences of ELL students in the classroom.

Teachers differentiating instruction for ELL students should carefully consider the needs of these students as they introduce and use academic language in various language domains (listening, speaking, reading, and writing) throughout this module. In order to adequately differentiate instruction for ELL students, teachers should have an understanding of the proficiency level of each student. WIDA provides an assessment tool to assist teachers in assessing English language proficiency levels at https://www.wida.us/assessment/access. The following 9–12 WIDA standards are relevant to this module:

> Standard 1: Social and instructional language. Focus on social behavior in group work and class discussions.

Standard 2: The language of language arts. Focus on forms of print, elements of text, picture books, comprehension strategies, main ideas/details, persuasive language, creating informational text, and editing and revising.

Standard 3: The language of mathematics. Focus on numbers and operations, patterns, number sense, measurement, strategies for problem solving.

Standard 4: The language of science. Focus on safety practices, magnetism, energy sources, scientific process, and scientific inquiry.

Standard 5: The language of social studies. Focus on change from past to present, historical events, resources, transportation, map reading, and location of objects and places.

SAFETY CONSIDERATIONS FOR THE ACTIVITIES IN THIS MODULE

There are no major concerns regarding safety during this module. In science, English language arts, and social studies, students will be accessing information using the internet. Care should be taken to protect students from accessing internet sites that are inappropriate. Your IT contact person can provide guidance for appropriate search engines. Additionally, they may already have protective measures in place to prevent the students from accessing inappropriate content. For more precautions, see the specific safety notes after the list of materials in each lesson. For more general safety guidelines, see the Safety in STEM section in Chapter 2 (p. 19).

DESIRED OUTCOMES AND MONITORING SUCCESS

The entire unit is intended to scaffold learning so that students learn necessary foundational information at the beginning of the unit that will be applied throughout the unit. The foundational understandings of time period categorizations such as Pleistocene and Holocene eras, learned in module one will provide students with the background information necessary to apply this information to the projects throughout the unit. Following module one, students are challenged to synthesize complex information related to the Earth's processes, and students will be required to communicate their argument regarding the potential boundary for the Anthropocene Era to professionals. Some students may be successful given only the desired outcomes, while other students may need scaffolding by providing benchmark goals along the way. Students can use these desired outcomes to self-monitor and check that they are progressing in a positive direction.

Table 3.3. Desired Outcomes and Evidence of Success

Desired Outcome	Evidence of Success in Achieving Identified Outcome	
To identify, define, and describe attributes of periods, eras, and epochs which have marked geologic time periods in Earth's history	Time scale chronology activity in which students successfully compile and arrange the assigned periods, eras, and epochs in chronological order	Slides connecting time scale to activity to Quaternary period which describe each periods, era, or epoch and serve as evidence for the time line
To evaluate various possible index layers and boundary events that mark the beginning of the Anthropocene Epoch to determine which is most appropriate when labeling the current period in Earth's history	Historical Analysis jigsaw activity that allows students to use the skills and habits of mind learned in the time scale activity toward Earth's most recent period. Using those practices, students will research more recent phenomena including plate tectonics, the biodiversity of the planet, acidification of the oceans, and glacial melting.	Successful sharing of "expert" knowledge gained in jigsaw research activity.
To design and present a multimedia presentation and textbook entry to share with textbook publishers regarding information on the Anthropocene to include in a secondary-level Earth science textbook	A multimedia presentation that includes specific characteristics from geologic principles applied to the current state of the Earth's formation	A textbook entry suitable for publication with text and images that demonstrates the student's understanding of geologic principles, interpretation of historical data, and effective writing practices

ASSESSMENT PLAN

Table 3.4 provides an overview of the major group and individual products and deliverables that comprise the assessment for this module. See Table 3.5 for a full assessment map of formative and summative assessments in this module.

Table 3.4. Major Products/Deliverables in Lead Disciplines – Group and Individual

Lesson	Major Group Products/ Deliverables	Major Individual Products/ Deliverables
1	Time scale chart presentation Quaternary Period connection slides	STEM Research Notebooks Google Earth activity
2	Human influences on natural processes jigsaw	STEM Research NotebooksIf, Then handout
3	Textbook publisher consultant presentation	STEM Research Notebooks Multimodal textbook entry

Table 3.5. Assessment Map for Formation of the Earth Module

Lesson	Assessment	Group/ Individual	Formative/ Summative	Lesson Objective Assessed
1	STEM Research Notebook *prompts*	Group / Individual	Formative	Explain how past geologic events shape current terrain.
1	Google Earth activity	Group	Formative	Describe land formations by features and formation characteristics. Estimate time to create landforms.
1	Time ScaleActivity and Presentation *rubric*	Group	Formative	Use knowledge of geologic time scale to identify themes of geologically significant events. Research geologic time period. Present research on geologic time period.
1	Quaternary Activity and Presentation *rubric*	Group	Formative	Connect geologic past to present through the concept of epochs. Present research on epochs.
2	STEM Research Notebook *prompts*	Group	Formative	Explain major geologic changes occurring on earth currently.
2	STEM Research Notebook *prompts*	Group	Formative	Explain how global climate affects the natural process of Earth.

Continued

Table 3.5. (*continued*)

Lesson	Assessment	Group/Individual	Formative/Summative	Lesson Objective Assessed
2	Jigsaw Activity *rubric*	Group	Formative	Research and explain topic (i.e., biodiversity, glacial melting, ocean acidification, plate tectonics, global population).
2	Expert Group Posters *performance task*	Group	Formative	Research chosen earth formation topic. Explain why scientists are interested in the topic and why the topic is important to people/organisms.
2	STEM Research Notebook *prompts*	Group	Formative	Recognize manifestations of anthropogenic climate change through analysis of oceanic and biodiversity data.
2	If Then... *performance task*	Individual	Summative	Hypothesize potential effects of the changing processes on Earth.
3	STEM Research Notebook *prompts*	Group	Formative	Explain how history has impacted the how the Earth works today.
3	Nature of Science Presentations *rubric*	Group	Formative	Research and describe the main ways scientists might research climate change.
3	Nature of History Presentations *rubric*	Group	Formative	Research and describe the main ways historians conduct their studies.
3	Publisher Presentations *rubric*	Group	Summative	Develop a comprehensive report proposing supporting evidence for a single time period for the boundary event between the Holocene and Anthropocene epochs. Use Engineering Design Process.
3	Textbook Entry *rubric*	Group	Summative	Create a sample textbook entry with text, figures, images, and/or graphs.

MODULE TIMELINE

Tables 3.6–3.10 (pp. 39–42) provide lesson timelines for each week of the module. These timelines are provided for general guidance only and are based on class times of approximately 45 minutes.

STEM ROAD MAP MODULE TIMELINE

Table 3.6. STEM Road Map Module Schedule Week One

Day 1	Day 2	Day 3	Day 4	Day 5
Lesson 1 *Geologic Time* Students are introduced to the unit with an interactive activity on Google Earth. History students will watch the "Big History" video. Expected Daily Outcome: Google Earth activity	*Lesson 1* *Geologic Time* Students are arranged into teams and assigned time periods. Groups begin research on their time period. Expected Daily Outcome: Data gathering document on characteristics of assigned time period	*Lesson 1* *Geologic Time* Student teams wrap up data collection and begin organizing the presentation. Expected Daily Outcome: Data gathering document on characteristics of assigned time period	*Lesson 1* *Geologic Time* Teams present data about the assigned time period and boundaries in chronological order. Expected Daily Outcome: Presentations of assigned period	*Lesson 1* *Geologic Time* Individuals research either the Pleistocene or Holocene and share out with partners. Pairs then discuss how their original time period affected the Quaternary and assemble a small (one-two slides) presentation to be added to the larger class presentation. Expected Daily Outcome: Presentation draft (Pleistocene or Holocene Epoch)

Table 3.7. STEM Road Map Module Schedule Week Two

Day 6	Day 7	Day 8	Day 9	Day 10
Lesson 1 *Geologic Time* Pairs present reasoning for the importance of their time period to the development of the Quaternary. Class discussion. Expected Daily Outcome: Final presentation slide(s) connecting assigned period to Pleistocene and Holocene Epochs	*Lesson 2* *Human Influences on Natural Processes* Students will present their models through a gallery walk and provide peer feedback.	*Lesson 2* *Human Influences on Natural Processes* Expert groups research topics and begin organizing major concepts related to human-influenced phenomena that characterize current Earth formation. Expected Daily Outcome: Expert group deliberation notes on human-involved phenomena	*Lesson 2* *Human Influences on Natural Processes* Students begin creating a poster board or similar artifact that will inform the rest of the class of their topic. Expected Daily Outcome: Expert group poster draft	*Lesson 2* *Human Influences on Natural Processes* Expert groups finalize poster. Original groups reconvene and posters are passed from group to group as the expert of each group shares his/her poster or artifact. Expected Daily Outcome: Final human influences on natural processes jigsaw presentation

Table 3.8. STEM Road Map Module Schedule Week Three

Day 11	Day 12	Day 13	Day 14	Day 15
Lesson 2 Human Influences on Natural Processes Groups discuss the human induced phenomena. Individuals complete the "If, Then" activity to hypothesize about the interconnectivity of the topics they researched. Expected Daily Outcome: Individual "If, Then" activity worksheet	*Lesson 3 The Anthropocene: Exploring and Deliberating a New Epoch in Geologic Time* Earth science and world history classes separately prepare for presentations to share with collaborators in order to describe the ways of knowing and habits of mind essential to their respective fields including historical thinking, understanding the nature of science, and using geologic evidence. Expected Daily Outcome: Presentation draft	*Lesson 3 The Anthropocene: Exploring and Deliberating a New Epoch in Geologic Time* Both science and world history classes come together to share ideas fundamental to thinking like a historian, the nature of science, and using geologic evidence. Interdisciplinary groups begin reviewing science textbooks to examine structure, formatting, and language use. Expected Daily Outcome: Share out presentations	*Lesson 3 The Anthropocene: Exploring and Deliberating a New Epoch in Geologic Time* History class presents Earth science class with information on major periods in human history under investigation for this project (e.g. the birth of agriculture, the Age of Exploration, the Industrial Revolution, the Great Acceleration, the Information Age). Expected Daily Outcome: History human history packets; Earth science notes on human history	*Lesson 3 The Anthropocene: Exploring and Deliberating a New Epoch in Geologic Time* Interdisciplinary groups discuss each time period in terms of historical significance and geologic impact on Earth's formation. Science students share their knowledge of the criteria for geologic boundaries and current Earth formation processes. Expected Daily Outcome: Individual's notes on Lessons 1 and 2

Table 3.9. STEM Road Map Module Schedule Week Four

Day 16	Day 17	Day 18	Day 19	Day 20
Lesson 3 *The Anthropocene: Exploring and Deliberating a New Epoch in Geologic Time* Groups utilize the graphic organizer to keep track of data and decide which period in human history most significantly marks the boundary for the Anthropocene Epoch. Groups also review presentation strategies and best practices in preparation for their presentation to textbook publisher. Expected Daily Outcome: Completed history graphic organizer	*Lesson 3* *The Anthropocene: Exploring and Deliberating a New Epoch in Geologic Time* From the deliberation on Day 16, interdisciplinary groups will begin to develop the presentation to the textbook publishers. Expected Daily Outcome: Presentation outline	*Lesson 3* *The Anthropocene: Exploring and Deliberating a New Epoch in Geologic Time* Continue presentation development for textbook publishers Expected Daily Outcome: Presentation draft	*Lesson 3* *The Anthropocene: Exploring and Deliberating a New Epoch in Geologic Time* Finalize presentations Expected Daily Outcome: Final presentation	*Lesson 3* *The Anthropocene: Exploring and Deliberating a New Epoch in Geologic Time* Presentation day 1 Expected Daily Outcome: Group presentations

Table 3.10. STEM Road Map Module Schedule Week Five

Day 21	Day 22	Day 23	Day 24	Day 25
Lesson 3 *The Anthropocene: Exploring and Deliberating a New Epoch in Geologic Time* Presentation day 2 and class debriefing Expected Daily Outcome: Group presentations	*Lesson 3* *The Anthropocene: Exploring and Deliberating a New Epoch in Geologic Time* Textbook entry writing which includes 2–3 paragraphs of text and at least three integrated figures or graphs. Expected Daily Outcome: Textbook entry draft	*Lesson 3* *The Anthropocene: Exploring and Deliberating a New Epoch in Geologic Time* Complete a final draft of textbook writing to be submitted to English and math class for editing Expected Daily Outcome: Textbook excerpt draft with integrated figures or graphs	*Lesson 3* *The Anthropocene: Exploring and Deliberating a New Epoch in Geologic Time* Complete and submit textbook excerpt Expected Daily Outcome: Final textbook excerpts	*Lesson 3* *The Anthropocene: Exploring and Deliberating a New Epoch in Geologic Time* Complete and submit textbook excerpt Expected Daily Outcome: Final textbook excerpts

RESOURCES

School-based Individuals: Teachers can opt to co-teach portions of this unit and may want to combine classes for activities such as establishing international partnerships, community mapping, and calculating energy usage. A Media Specialist can help teachers locate resources.

Technology: Internet access; a shared space to post and re-work multimodal presentations.

Materials: Internet resources; graphic organizers to support students making connections across topics and making inferences.

REFERENCES

Peters-Burton, E. E., Seshaiyer, P., Burton, S. R., Drake-Patrick, J., and Johnson, C. C. 2015. The STEM road map for grades 9-12. In C. C. Johnson, E. E. Peters-Burton, and T. J. Moore (Eds.), *STEM road map: A framework for integrated STEM education* (pp. 124–162). New York, NY: Routledge.

WIDA Consortium. 2012. 2012 Amplification of the English language development standards: Kindergarten-grade 12. Retrieved from https://www.wida.us/standards/eld.aspx

FORMATION OF
THE EARTH – LESSON PLANS

*Anthony Pellegrino, Emily Bird, Erin E. Peters-Burton, Jennifer Drake Patrick,
Bradley D. Rankin, Susan Poland, Janet B. Walton, and Carla C. Johnson*

Lesson Plan 1:
Geologic Time: An Introduction to the Geologic Time Scale and How Its Boundaries are Defined

LESSON ONE SUMMARY

In this lesson, students will begin by exploring the Earth's geologic features and hypothesizing how these features manifested. From those hypotheses, students will be introduced to the geologic time scale and how it is divided into eons, eras, periods, and epochs. Students will apply understanding of geologically significant events to discern what constitutes geologic boundaries and what characteristics define these events. In this lesson, groups of 2–3 students will be assigned a specific period in geologic time and tasked with illustrating characteristics of their time period, including boundaries on either side (when applicable). The whole class will then arrange their time periods in chronological order identifying the common boundary events they discerned and deliberating regarding these events. This will become a class timeline of Earth's history.

ESSENTIAL QUESTION(S)

Why do humans set out to define and describe various periods in Earth's formation?

What are some examples of events that would indicate a new eon, era, period, or epoch?

What defines these events and what are the attributes and non-attributes?

ESTABLISHED GOALS/OBJECTIVES

At the conclusion of this lesson, students will be able to:

- describe the concept of stratigraphy and how it is used to correlate geologic time;

- explain how plate tectonics greatly influence Earth's characteristics;
- use knowledge of geologic time scale to identify themes of geologically significant events.

TIME REQUIRED

6 days (approximately 45 minutes each; Days 1–6 in the schedule)

NECESSARY MATERIALS

Internet access for research

Google Earth

Access to presentation software such as PowerPoint or Prezi

Table 4.1. Content Standards Addressed in STEM Road Map Module Lesson One

---

NEXT GENERATION SCIENCE STANDARDS

PERFORMANCE EXPECTATIONS

HS-ESS1–6 Apply scientific reasoning and evidence from ancient Earth materials, meteorites, and other planetary surfaces to construct an account of Earth's formation and early history.

HS-ESS2–1 Develop a model to illustrate how Earth's internal and surface processes operate at different spatial and temporal scales to form continental and ocean-floor features.

HS-ESS2–2 Analyze geoscience data to make the claim that one change to Earth's surface can create feedbacks that cause changes to other Earth systems.

HS-LS2–1 Use mathematical and/or computational representations to support explanations of factors that affect carrying capacity of ecosystems at different scales.

DISCIPLINARY CORE IDEAS

ESS1.C: The History of Planet Earth

Although active geologic processes, such as plate tectonics and erosion, have destroyed or altered most of the very early rock record on Earth, other objects in the solar system, such as lunar rocks, asteroids, and meteorites, have changed little over billions of years. Studying these objects can provide information about Earth's formation and early history.

PS1.C: Nuclear Processes

Spontaneous radioactive decays follow a characteristic exponential decay law. Nuclear lifetimes allow radiometric dating to be used to determine the ages of rocks and other materials. (secondary)

ESS2.A: Earth Materials and Systems

Earth's systems, being dynamic and interacting, cause feedback effects that can increase or decrease the original changes.

ESS2.B: Plate Tectonics and Large-Scale System Interactions

Plate tectonics is the unifying theory that explains the past and current movements of the rocks at Earth's surface and provides a framework for understanding its geologic history. Plate movements are responsible for most continental and ocean-floor features and for the distribution of most rocks and minerals within Earth's crust. (ESS2.B Grade 8 GBE)

ESS2.D: Weather and Climate

The foundation for Earth's global climate systems is the electromagnetic radiation from the sun, as well as its reflection, absorption, storage, and redistribution among the atmosphere, ocean, and land systems, and this energy's re-radiation into space.

LS2.A: Interdependent Relationships in Ecosystems

Ecosystems have carrying capacities, which are limits to the numbers of organisms and populations they can support. These limits result from such factors as the availability of living and nonliving resources and from such challenges such as predation, competition, and disease. Organisms would have the capacity to produce populations of great size were it not for the fact that environments and resources are finite. This fundamental tension affects the abundance (number of individuals) of species in any given ecosystem.

CROSSCUTTING CONCEPTS

Stability and Change

Much of science deals with constructing explanations of how things change and how they remain stable.

Change and rates of change can be quantified and modeled over very short or very long periods of time. Some system changes are irreversible.

Feedback (negative or positive) can stabilize or destabilize a system.

Scale, Proportion, and Quantity

The significance of a phenomenon is dependent on the scale, proportion, and quantity at which it occurs.

- -

Connections to Engineering, Technology, and Applications of Science

Influence of Engineering, Technology, and Science on Society and the Natural World

New technologies can have deep impacts on society and the environment, including some that were not anticipated. Analysis of costs and benefits is a critical aspect of decisions about technology.

Continued

Table 4.1. (*continued*)

SCIENCE AND ENGINEERING PRACTICES

Constructing Explanations and Designing Solutions

Constructing explanations and designing solutions in 9–12 builds on K–8 experiences and progresses to explanations and designs that are supported by multiple and independent student-generated sources of evidence consistent with scientific ideas, principles, and theories.

Apply scientific reasoning to link evidence to the claims to assess the extent to which the reasoning and data support the explanation or conclusion.

Developing and Using Models

Modeling in 9–12 builds on K–8 experiences and progresses to using, synthesizing, and developing models to predict and show relationships among variables between systems and their components in the natural and designed world(s).

Develop a model based on evidence to illustrate the relationships between systems or between components of a system.

Analyzing and Interpreting Data

Analyzing data in 9–12 builds on K–8 experiences and progresses to introducing more detailed statistical analysis, the comparison of data sets for consistency, and the use of models to generate and analyze data.

Analyze data using tools, technologies, and/or models (e.g., computational, mathematical) in order to make valid and reliable scientific claims or determine an optimal design solution.

- -

Connections to Nature of Science

Science Models, Laws, Mechanisms, and Theories Explain Natural Phenomena

A scientific theory is a substantiated explanation of some aspect of the natural world, based on a body of facts that have been repeatedly confirmed through observation and experiment and the science community validates each theory before it is accepted. If new evidence is discovered that the theory does not accommodate, the theory is generally modified in light of this new evidence.

Models, mechanisms, and explanations collectively serve as tools in the development of a scientific theory.

COMMON CORE MATHEMATICS STANDARDS

MATHEMATICS PRACTICES

MP1 Make sense of problems and persevere in solving them.

MP3 Construct viable arguments and critique the reasoning of others.

MP5 Use appropriate tools strategically.

MP6 Attend to precision.

MP8 Look for and express regularity in repeated reasoning.

Mathematics Content

HSN.Q.A.1 Use units as a way to understand problems and to guide the solution of multi-step problems; choose and interpret units consistently in formulas; choose and interpret the scale and the origin in graphs and data displays.

HSN-Q.A.2 Define appropriate quantities for the purpose of descriptive modeling.

HSS-ID.A.1 Represent data with plots on the real number line.

COMMON CORE ENGLISH LANGUAGE ARTS STANDARDS

WRITING STANDARDS

W.9–10.1a Introduce precise claim(s), distinguish the claim(s) from alternate or opposing claims, and create an organization that establishes clear relationships among claim(s), counterclaims, reasons, and evidence.

W.9–10.1b Develop claim(s) and counterclaims fairly, supplying evidence for each while pointing out the strengths and limitations of both in a manner that anticipates the audience's knowledge level and concerns.

W.9–10.1c Use words, phrases, and clauses to link the major sections of the text, create cohesion, and clarify the relationships between claim(s) and reasons, between reasons and evidence, and between claim(s) and counterclaims.

W.9–10.1d Establish and maintain a formal style and objective tone while attending to the norms and conventions of the discipline in which they are writing.

W.9–10.1e Provide a concluding statement or section that follows from and supports the argument presented.

W.9–10.2a Introduce a topic; organize complex ideas, concepts, and information to make important connections and distinctions; include formatting (e.g., headings), graphics (e.g., figures, tables), and multimedia when useful to aiding comprehension.

W.9–10.2b Develop the topic with well-chosen, relevant, and sufficient facts, extended definitions, concrete details, quotations, or other information and examples appropriate to the audience's knowledge of the topic.

W.9–10.2c Use appropriate and varied transitions to link the major sections of the text, create cohesion, and clarify the relationships among complex ideas and concepts.

W.9–10.2d Use precise language and domain-specific vocabulary to manage the complexity of the topic.

W.9–10.2e Establish and maintain a formal style and objective tone while attending to the norms and conventions of the discipline in which they are writing.

W.9–10.2f Provide a concluding statement or section that follows from and supports the information or explanation presented (e.g., articulating implications or the significance of the topic).

Continued

Table 4.1. (*continued*)

> W.9–10.4 Produce clear and coherent writing in which the development, organization, and style are appropriate to task, purpose, and audience.
>
> W.9–10.6 Use technology, including the Internet, to produce, publish, and update individual or shared writing products, taking advantage of technology's capacity to link to other information and to display information flexibly and dynamically.
>
> W.9–10.8 Gather relevant information from multiple authoritative print and digital sources, using advanced searches effectively; assess the usefulness of each source in answering the research question; integrate information into the text selectively to maintain the flow of ideas, avoiding plagiarism and following a standard format for citation.
>
> W.9–10.10 Write routinely over extended time frames (time for research, reflection, and revision) and shorter time frames (a single sitting or a day or two) for a range of tasks, purposes, and audiences.
>
> **21ST CENTURY SKILLS**
>
> Leadership and Responsibility Learning and Innovation, 21st Century Interdisciplinary Skills, Information Media and Technology Skills, Life and Career Skills

Table 4.2. Key Vocabulary in Lesson One

Key Vocabulary*	Definition
Stratum (Strata)	Layer(s) of rock with distinguishing characteristics
Stratigraphy	The study of the order and relative position of strata and their relationship to geologic time
Boundary Event	A geologically significant event that changes the characteristics of Earth
Index Layer	Stratum that is used to define a specific period in geologic time such as a boundary event
Geologic Time Scale	A scale of time from the formation of Earth to the present. Scientists organize this scale into divisions of time which are, from largest to smallest: eons, eras, periods, and epochs. These classifications have no standards in terms of number of years, but are delineated by major geologic and biologic events.
Plate tectonics	Theory of the movement of the Earth's crust due to convection in the mantle
Biodiversity	The variety of life in the world or in a particular ecosystem
Climate	The weather conditions prevailing in an area in general or over a long period

Table 4.2. (*continued*)

Key Vocabulary*	Definition
Pangaea	A supercontinent that incorporated nearly all of Earth's land masses that was completely assembled at the end of the Carboniferous Period, approximately 300 million years ago. Pangaea began to break up at the end of the Triassic Period, 200 million years ago.
Global Climate	A generalized description of the climate over the entire Earth. This term typically refers to the Earth's state of glaciation at a particular time.
Mass Extinction	When one or more species becomes extinct due to a major event, such as a meteor impact or major volcanic eruptions.

* Vocabulary terms are provided for both teacher and student use. Teachers may choose to introduce all or some terms to students.

TEACHER BACKGROUND INFORMATION

The teacher should understand the geologic time scale and how boundary events such as mass extinctions occurred. The teacher should comprehend the cause and effect nature of major geologic events. For review and reference, a simplified geologic time scale is included in the following material (see Resource B). Major events include but are not limited to: critical developments in Earth's biodiversity (evolution or extinction of a species), significant results of plate tectonics, and major fluctuations in global climate. In this lesson the teacher should guide students towards an understanding of plate tectonics and how it can affect global climate as well as biodiversity. The teacher should also introduce the concept of stratigraphy and how scientists use layers of rock to pinpoint moments in geologic time.

Students will be grappling with ideas such as significance, chronology, and change and continuity over time and how they mesh with the much larger time scale they are dealing with in this lesson. For teachers unfamiliar with these concepts, teachinghistory. org offers an informative introductory video (http://teachinghistory.org/historical-thinking-intro). The Historical Thinking Project provides a useful delineation of fundamental concepts related to historical thinking including those listed above

LESSON PREPARATION

In preparation for the Google Earth activity, the teacher should introduce students to concepts such as Pangaea, global climate, and mass extinctions. Additionally, video and images of volcanoes and natural erosion processes will help the students imagine these processes as they examine the geologic features they are assigned in this introductory activity.

For the group time scale activity, the teacher will divide the students into groups of two or three and assign each group a period on the geologic time scale from the

Precambrian to the Neogene (all students will address the current Quaternary Period in this activity). Before the lesson, the teacher should review the simplified geologic time scale we have provided and become familiar with the major events associated with each period to better guide the students towards meaningful characteristics.

It is suggested that teachers split the Quaternary Period into its two epochs (Pleistocene and Holocene) to allow students to further explore the various classifications of time. In their original groups, each student will independently focus on one of the epochs of the Quaternary and share out with his or her partner(s) to gain a collective understanding of the period. The class will then debate on which individual's time period was most significant to the development of the Quaternary Period.

LEARNING PLAN COMPONENTS
Introductory Activity/Engagement
Science Class

Connections to the Challenge: Begin each day of this lesson by directing students' attention to the driving question for the module and challenge, asking "Why is it critical to understand "big history" before we can comprehend the present?" Hold a brief student discussion of how their learning in the previous days' lesson(s) contributed to their ability to create their innovation for the final challenge. You may wish to hold a class discussion, creating a class list of key ideas on chart paper or the board, or you may wish to have students create a STEM Research Notebook entry with this information.

STEM Research Notebook Prompt

What do you think is meant by "Big History?"

How does the human experience compare to the origins of life on Earth?

How does the human experience compare to the origins of the universe?

Do you think humans as a species are powerful? Why or why not?

Students should record their thoughts in their STEM Research Notebook and consider what is meant by "big history," how past geologic events shape current terrain and therefore, the life that we live. Guide students to think about these concepts as necessary as you rotate around the room as they write downs their thoughts. Facilitate a whole class discussion and record key points on the board for the group, then students should record key discussion points in their STEM research notebooks.

In preparation for the interdisciplinary of this unit, students should watch the "What is Big History?" video (https://www.youtube.com/watch?v=4VICS9cIugo). Mathematics and social studies principles are particularly evident here and may be included in science class as appropriate depending on the level of collaboration with the other core content teachers.

In the opening activity, students will use Google Earth or other similar satellite sites to explore several features of the planet that are present as a result of formation processes. Specifically, students will focus on landforms that are the result of plate tectonics, such as the puzzle-piece shapes of the continents, mountain ranges, the Pacific "Ring of Fire" or actively rifting areas like the Mid-Atlantic Ridge or the Red Sea. Students may write about/speculate how those came about and how long those processes took. They may use a graphic organizer to help make appropriate connections between the features about which they choose to write. A handout that might help guide students' thinking throughout this activity is included at the end of this lesson one.

Mathematics Connections

Students should review time scale data to assist with the writing activity from science class.

These data are available as a handout at the end of this lesson.

Putting the scale of dates in context will help students comprehend the enormous lengths of time between eras, periods, and epochs. Use this video by National Public Radio as an introduction to explain how a 100 yard football field can be used to explain the Earth's history by using 1 inch to represent 1.3 million years. There are many websites that visualize the history of the universe that may be helpful in first understanding the scope and scale of the timeline. This is an example of a timeline of the universe that includes the death of the sun in the future from the website Science Alert https://www.sciencealert.com/timeline-shows-the-entire-history-of-the-universe-and-how-it-ends.

Students should use these data to make their own analogy of Earth's evolution. Students can work individually or in groups of 2 or 3 to create a poster representing their timeline. The following website uses a football analogy mathematics teachers can use to illustrate Earth's evolution: https://signalvnoise.com/images/grs02_03.gif

Using the number of yards an eon, era, period, or epoch represents, students can compare these yards to the 100-yard-length that is Earth's age. Students should present their timelines to the class. Audience members in the class should ask clarifying questions about how the analogy compares to the formation of the Earth.

ELA Connections

In the opening activity, students use Google Earth (https://www.google.com/earth/) or other similar satellite sites to explore several features of the planet that are present as a result of formation processes. Specifically, students will focus on landforms that are the result of plate tectonics, such as the puzzle-piece shapes of the continents, mountain ranges, or actively rifting areas like the Mid-Atlantic Ridge or the Red Sea. Students should take this tutorial on Geological Features on Planet Earth before they begin https://www.sophia.org/tutorials/exploring-geological-features-using-google-earth. This tutorial shows how to tag geological features on the Earth and enter questions that students might have about the formation of the different features. Students may write about/speculate how those came about and how long those processes took. Students should form a question which they explore using Google Earth and record it in their notebooks. Students should then "tinker" with Google Earth to find visual relationships to help them answer their questions. Ask students to develop a written hypothesis connecting the feature(s) on which they focus in the Google Earth activity. A product from this activity may include an explanation of how the Mid-Atlantic Ridge affects the continents to its east and west, for example. To look at features on the seafloor, students may need to embed an overlay. Directions to take an expedition to the Earth's Seafloor can be found here http://joidesresolution.org/wp-content/uploads/2018/03/Google-Earth-Seafloor_Teacher.pdf.

An example graphic organizer that students can create in their STEM Research Notebooks is found below. The intention is to not fully investigate the questions in this portion of the lesson, but to motivate students to explore and broaden their thinking about the formation of the Earth.

Question that can be investigated on Google Earth

Review each of the following landforms using Google Earth. Based on your careful examination of each, speculate on the following:

- What is striking about this landform?
- What do you know about its formation?
- How does this feature relate to the landforms around it?
- Estimate the time it took to create this landform

Himalayas

Shapes of Continents

Mid-Atlantic Ridge

Red Sea

Baja Mexico

Alaskan Aleutian Islands

Social Studies Connections

Students should watch the "What is Big History?" video (https://www.youtube.com/watch?v=4VICS9cIugo) and formulate ideas regarding how the study of geologic time supports and challenges principles of historical thinking. After they watch the video ask students to get into pairs and discuss the following STEM Research Notebook prompts, writing down important ideas that are discussed in the pairs for each question:

Should humans be the centerpiece for historical explanation?

Are humans the most significant thing that have happened in recent history?

What is the best way to explain the chronology of the formation of the universe and the earth in a way that is understandable?

What are some features that you think have stayed the same over the time in the history of the universe?

What are some features that you think have changed over the time in the history of the universe?

Students should grapple with ideas such as significance, chronology, and change and continuity over time and how they mesh with the much larger time scale they are dealing with in this lesson.

As a whole class, conduct a discussion of student answers and help students connect their responses to the challenge. Students will be creating a multimedia presentation to argue for the presence of the Anthropocene Era (an era where humans have influenced climate) into materials that schools will adopt for teaching. Student ideas about humans' place and influence on the Earth in their answers will be the starting points for the material they will use for their challenge.

ACTIVITY/INVESTIGATION
Science Class

Following the Google activity on day one, pairs of students will be assigned a geologic time period which they will research (included at the end of this lesson). Using the data collection guide (included at the end of this lesson), students will investigate and compile information about defining characteristics and boundary events for their time period. In particular, students are tasked with uncovering the major scientific evidence used to determine the beginning and endings of major geologic time periods. Students are encouraged to consult many resources to find this information, including books,

online resources, natural history museums, or even local researchers who might be willing to assist with this project.

Mathematics Connections

Students create ratios of time using the football field analogy activity. Examples for how to calculate ratios for the analogy is found below

$$\frac{\text{Known age of past event in years}}{\text{Known age of the earth in years}} = \frac{\text{Unknown Time Scale analogy result}}{\text{Maximum measurement in analogy}}$$

Students can work in pairs to complete this activity. After calculating ratios in pairs, students should share their findings with one another. Students will likely note that ratios can be calculated in different ways and represented in different ways (fractions or percentages). The teacher should facilitate discussion, acknowledging that either way of representing the ratios can be considered correct. The teacher should also direct students to consider patterns in the ratios, noting that the ratios have not been consistent over geologic time.

ELA Connections

Students will have the opportunity to read fiction and nonfiction information about the time period under investigation to inform the presentation. *The Cambrian Explosion* by Douglas Erwin, *A New History of Life* by Peter Ward, and *Earth Before the Dinosaurs* by Sébastien Steyer are three highly regarded non-fiction texts that cover many of these periods. *Legends of the Earth: Their Geologic Origins* by Dorothy Vitaliano includes a variety of myths from various cultures on the origin of the Earth. Additionally, the National Science Teachers Association (NSTA) publishes its "Outstanding Tradebooks" list each year (see http://www.nsta.org/publications/ostb/). This resource may also have some relevant titles.

Students will look at climate maps and almanac data to discern potential areas of the globe that may be manifestations of phenomena related to the formation of the Earth. Focusing on the history of the Appalachian or Ural Mountains, for example, may help students better understand geologic time over the course of many years, while looking at the more active Ring of Fire may demonstrate recent changes in geology. Teachers can emphasize that the geologic events that are currently occurring around the world help scientists to understand what has happened in the past. Scientists and historians work under the assumption that the geologic processes that are taking place on Earth today are very similar to the processes that took place millions/billions of years ago.

EXPLAIN

Science Class

Students should continue work started on Days 2 and 3 by continuing work in pairs. Students should work with the data collected on days two and three to develop a cohesive overview of their assigned time period. With the support of the other content areas, they will create a presentation consisting of three illustrated slides including two characteristics of the time period and one boundary event for their time period. Student presentations should be arranged in geologic time order. Students should record main concepts and key pieces of information in their STEM research notebooks to reference later. Presentations should be tailored to the assessment rubric provided at the end of this lesson, but presentations should be short enough to be fit into the time allotted. Depending on the number of students in the class, the teacher may be required to develop presentations on any time periods that students did not present.

Mathematics Connections

At many boundary events, mass extinctions have occurred. Using the time scale data from the time scale resource and outside resources, students should explore percentages of extinctions as evidence of boundary events/periods. Students should consider both plant and animal life, found on land or in water, and talk about why percentages of species lost are more easily understood than raw numbers of species lost. This is because it is hard to relate to a number of species without knowing the number of species currently living on earth, which is data that very few people know. Instead, percentages allow us to think about what it would be like if a percentage of all species died today and how that would impact life as we know it. Any data collected through this activity should be included in relevant student presentations on a particular time period.

ELA Connections

Students will learn about creating effective presentations and use these principles in the development of the timeline slides (see http://blog.ted.com/10-tips-for-better-slide-decks/). Students should consider who their audience is, how much time they are allotted for their presentations, and how they can present data in different ways in order to most effectively convey their findings.

Social Studies Connections

Students will work to ensure appropriate historical terms and ideas of historical thinking are included in the presentation drafts.

EXTEND/APPLY KNOWLEDGE
Science Class

The class will complete the Quaternary Period activity to explore the concept of epochs by studying the two most recent epochs, both of which involve humans. Doing so will help students connect the geologic past to present day. Remind students that in the football analogy, this involves approximately the last foot of a football field in relation to the beginnings of the universe.

Students should consider how their assigned geologic time period (from their presentations on Days 2–4) fits into the development of the Pleistocene or Holocene epochs. Students should choose to focus on either the Pleistocene or Holocene epochs. Students should research the boundary events of the Pleistocene or Holocene and record any findings in their STEM Research Notebooks. Students should then create one or two presentation slides that address how their time period fits with the Pleistocene or Holocene. Students will add these slides to a class presentation, organized chronologically.

On Day 6, students will take turns presenting their slides in the larger class presentation on how their time period fits with these recent epochs. By the end of the presentation, all time periods should be addressed relevant to the Pleistocene or Holocene, with the teacher filling in any gaps in time if there are not enough student pairs to address all time periods. Students should record main findings during their presentations in their STEM Research Notebooks.

Additionally, students will read two articles:

What is the Anthropocene and are we in it? From Smithsonian Magazine

- https://www.smithsonianmag.com/science-nature/what-is-the-anthropocene-and-are-we-in-it-164801414/

Is the Anthropocene an issue of stratigraphy or pop culture? In GSA Today

- http://www.geosociety.org/gsatoday/archive/22/7/article/i1052-5173-22-7-60.htm

related to the debate about the Anthropocene Epoch. Students should work in pairs, with one student reading one article and the other reading a second article, and then students should discuss the content of the article. This will serve as an introduction to the debate and support student learning of the markers of the Quaternary Period and its epochs. Teachers are encouraged to select the articles that are appropriate for students with different reading levels. After students read these articles in pairs, the class should have a discussion about the major claims made by each author. The format for the class discussion will be a circle discussion. When the pairs are finished reading

the articles and explaining them to each other, ask students to form an inner and outer circle. The students who form the inner circle should be experts on the Smithsonian article, and the students who form the outer circle should be experts on the GSA Today article. Ask the students in the inner circle to try to explain all of the major ideas from the article to their counterparts in the outer circle and vice versa. After one round of back and forth convincing, ask students to summarize the main points as you keep track of them on the board. Students should record main points from this debate in their STEM Research Notebooks.

Mathematics Connections

None for this portion of the lesson.

ELA Connections

Students should work in small groups (3–4 students) to dissect the two articles read in science class to discuss the validity of claims, evidence and reasoning made. More advanced students can analyze the article for any rebuttals. Students can use the graphic organizer found at the end of the lesson to analyze the article (Argumentation Graphic Organizer).

Each group should have all two articles and should compare and contrast all two articles. Students should focus on the language used by the different authors, considering who the intended audience is, and whether the article is easy to understand or difficult to read. Students should evaluate the claims and consider where the authors may have used faulty logic or made misleading claims. After working in small groups, the teacher should lead a group discussion on students' findings. Students can record the major ideas for communication to use in the future challenge in Lesson Three.

Social Studies Connections

None for this portion of the lesson

EVALUATE/ASSESSMENT

Performance Tasks:

Google Earth Activity (Day 1)

Time Scale Activity (Days 2–4)

Quaternary Activity (Days 5–6)

Attached at the end of the lesson are resources to support the teacher in guiding and assessing student outcomes on the performance tasks.

INTERNET RESOURCES

https://www.youtube.com/watch?v=4VICS9cIugo A seven-minute introduction to Big History with David Christian.

https://www.youtube.com/watch?v=M8V_glRW1hA A widely used football field analogy for time scale perspective.

http://www.earthsciweek.org/classroom-activities/geologic-time-scale-analogy A timescale classroom activity example from Earth Science Week

http://teachinghistory.org/historical-thinking-intro An introduction to Historical Thinking from the Roy Rosenzweig Center for History and New Media at George Mason University

http://blog.ted.com/10-tips-for-better-slide-decks/ A blog from the TED website outlining presentation best practices

http://www.smithsonianmag.com/science-nature/what-is-the-anthropocene-and-are-we-in-it-164801414/?no-ist A brief article from The Smithsonian Magazine outlining the debate over whether or not we are in the Anthropocene Epoch.

http://www.geosociety.org/gsatoday/archive/22/7/article/i1052-5173-22-7-60.htm A brief article from academic Whitney Autin in GSA Today questioning the label of Anthropocene.

http://www.economist.com/node/18744401 An article from The Economist Magazine outlining reasons why we should consider ourselves living in a new epoch.

Name:_____Date:_____

GOOGLE EARTH ACTIVITY

Review each of the following landforms using Google Earth. Based on your careful examination of each, speculate on the following:

- What is striking about this landform?

- What do you know about its formation?

- How does this feature relate to the landforms around it?

- Estimate the time it took to create this landform

Himalayas

Shapes of Continents

Mid-Atlantic Ridge

Red Sea

Baja Mexico

Alaskan Aleutian Islands

Time Scale Chart and Data Collection Guide

Name	Years	General Characteristics
Precambrian Eon	4.6 Billion-550 millions of years ago (mya)	• oxygenation of planet • origin of multicellular organisms
Cambrian Period	550–485 mya	• first appearance of animals with hard parts • no terrestrial life
Ordovician Period	485–445 mya	• first land plants • diverse marine life
Silurian Period	445–420 mya	• first spiders, scorpions, early insects
Devonian Period	420–360 mya	• first amphibians • diversification of marine and terrestrial life
Carboniferous Period	360–300 mya	• formation of Pangaea • first reptiles • early winged insects • appearance of cockroaches
Permian Period	300–250 mya	• appearance of beetles • amphibians dominate MASS EXTINCTION: 95% marine species 50% terrestrial species
Triassic Period	250–200 mya	• origin of mammals, dinosaurs, and flies • commencement of breakup of Pangaea
Jurassic Period	200–145 mya	• dinosaurs dominate the land • appearance of birds
Cretaceous Period	145–66 mya	• marsupials, butterflies, bees appear MASS EXTINCTION: 80% of all species
Paleogene Period	66–23 mya	• India collides with Asia • appearance and rapid abundance of mammals
Neogene Period	23–2.6 mya	• closure of isthmus of Panama • evolution of flowering plants • dogs and bears appear • first hominids
Quaternary Period*	2.6 mya-present	• first modern humans • major glaciation event • appearance of civilization • extinction of large mammals
Pleistocene Epoch*	2.6 mya-11,000 years ago	• appearance of modern humans • major glaciation
Holocene Epoch*	11,000 years ago-present	• extinction of large mammals in northern hemisphere • evolution of civilization

*See Lesson Preparation above for instruction related to these time periods.

Data Collection Guide – How Scientists Have Determined Major Geologic Periods

Use this form to record data that scientists have collected over time in order to determine the beginning and ends of geologic time periods.

Type of data collected	Source of data	When were these data collected?	From whom do these data come?	Questions these data will answer

NATIONAL SCIENCE TEACHING ASSOCIATION

Argumentation Graphic Organizer

Problem/Question:

⇩

Original Claim:

⇩

	Evidence	Reasoning
1		
2		
3		

⇩

Evidence Number	Rebuttal	Valid	Rationale

⇩

Conclusion:

Lesson One Presentation Rubric

	Expert	Competent	Emerging	Did not meet expectations	Score
Evidence of Data Collection	Data presented in presentation was directly related to energy consumption and climate change in local/regional areas and background knowledge was correctly cited.	Data presented in presentation was directly related to energy consumption and climate change in local/regional areas. Limited background knowledge was cited.	Data presented in presentation was not directly related to energy consumption and climate change in local/regional areas. Any data presented were not connected to background knowledge.	Little or no data were presented. No evidence of using outside sources to inform blog posting	
Data Organization	Data were clearly organized and connected to the topic throughout the blog posting	Data were clearly organized, but connections between topics was limited throughout the blog posting	Data were minimally organized. No connections between topics was evident	Data were not organized systematically.	
Presentation of Information	Results and conclusion were constructed as an argument, supported clearly by evidence and reasoning found in the data collection	Results and conclusion were communicated, but not constructed as an argument, supported clearly by evidence and reasoning found in the data collection	Results were communicated, but a conclusion was not constructed	Neither results nor conclusion were communicated	

Lesson Plan 2
Human Influences on Natural Processes: Climate Change, Biodiversity, and the World's Oceans

LESSON TWO SUMMARY

During this lesson students will gain an understanding of natural and anthropogenic processes on Earth. This lesson is designed to explain natural processes that affected Earth's formation and introduce the concept of human-induced climate change and the consequential changes to Earth's natural processes. Students will find information and collect data on plate tectonics, the biodiversity of the planet, acidification of the oceans, and glacial melting to further understand how increasing temperatures in combination with an expanding global population is affecting the Earth. Additionally, students will recognize that major events in these processes are geologically significant. This lesson serves as a connection between Lessons one and three in that students learn about the phenomena that affect the processes learned about in Lesson one. The activities in lesson two support students' conceptual understanding and the deliberative skills they will use in Lesson Three when they research and select the boundary that delineates the Anthropocene Epoch.

Essential Question(s)

> How do natural processes like plate tectonics affect Earth's temperature, biodiversity, and pH levels of the oceans?

> What evidence exists that current climate change is anthropogenic? How has anthropogenic climate change affected these characteristics?

> What are the consequences of these major changes as they relate to one another?

Established Goals/Objectives

At the conclusion of this lesson, students will be able to:

- interpret human-influenced processes on Earth;

- recognize manifestations of anthropogenic climate change through analysis of oceanic and biodiversity data;

- analyze major changes in ocean acidity, biodiversity, and global temperature and how these changes signify geologic significant events.

Time Required

5 days (approximately 45 minutes each; Days 7–11 in schedule)

Necessary Materials

Internet access for research, poster paper and other supplies for presenting and displaying around the classroom.

Extension Opportunity

While interdisciplinarity is encouraged throughout this unit, collaborating with world history, ELA, and mathematics teachers may be even more beneficial and worthwhile for the final two lessons of this PBL unit. Math will be critical to these lessons to help disaggregate data related to plate tectonics, the biodiversity of the planet, acidification of the oceans, and glacial melting to further understand how increasing temperatures in combination with an expanding global population are affecting the Earth. ELA teachers and students will support the final two lessons by focusing on communication of ideas in final presentations as well as augmenting the presentations with ideas coming from texts related to the formation of the Earth.

Additionally, consider arranging interdisciplinary groups of history and Earth science students for the final two lessons. Doing so will allow history students to learn about "big history" concepts and Earth science students to learn about the specific periods under consideration as the boundary (birth of agriculture, the Age of Exploration, Industrial Revolution, the Great Acceleration, the Information Age) for the Anthropocene Epoch. For example, during this lesson history students learn from Earth science students about the historical arc of the Earth's geologic periods and the changes that characterize each. The history students will provide an analytic understanding of studying the past and can offer support to Earth science students in how to define and interpret events/periods under consideration as the boundary for the Anthropocene Epoch. Together, the interdisciplinary groups can develop the final artifacts.

Table 4.3. Standards Addressed in STEM Road Map Module Lesson Two

NEXT GENERATION SCIENCE STANDARDS
PERFORMANCE EXPECTATIONS
HS-ESS2–1 Develop a model to illustrate how Earth's internal and surface processes operate at different spatial and temporal scales to form continental and ocean-floor features.
HS-ESS2–7 Construct an argument based on evidence about the simultaneous coevolution of Earth's systems and life on Earth.
HS-ESS3–1 Construct an explanation based on evidence for how the availability of natural, occurrence of natural hazards, and changes in climate have influenced human activity.

DISCIPLINARY CORE IDEAS

ESS2.A: Earth Materials and Systems

Earth's systems, being dynamic and interacting, cause feedback effects that can increase or decrease the original changes.

ESS2.B: Plate Tectonics and Large-Scale System Interactions

Plate tectonics is the unifying theory that explains the past and current movements of the rocks at Earth's surface and provides a framework for understanding its geologic history. Plate movements are responsible for most continental and ocean-floor features and for the distribution of most rocks and minerals within Earth's crust. (ESS2.B Grade 8 GBE)

ESS2.D: Weather and Climate

The foundation for Earth's global climate systems is the electromagnetic radiation from the sun, as well as its reflection, absorption, storage, and redistribution among the atmosphere, ocean, and land systems, and this energy's re-radiation into space.

ESS2.E Biogeology

The many dynamic and delicate feedbacks between the biosphere and other Earth systems cause a continual co-evolution of Earth's surface and the life that exists on it.

ESS3.A: Natural Resources

Resource availability has guided the development of human society.

ESS3.B: Natural Hazards

Natural hazards and other geologic events have shaped the course of human history; [they] have significantly altered the sizes of human populations and have driven human migrations.

CROSSCUTTING CONCEPTS

Stability and Change

Change and rates of change can be quantified and modeled over very short or very long periods of time. Some system changes are irreversible.

Cause and Effect

Empirical evidence is required to differentiate between cause and correlation and make claims about specific causes and effects.

Connections to Engineering, Technology, and Applications of Science

Influence of Science, Engineering, and Technology on Society and the Natural World Modern civilization depends on major technological systems.

SCIENCE AND ENGINEERING PRACTICES

Developing and Using Models

Modeling in 9–12 builds on K–8 experiences and progresses to using, synthesizing, and developing models to predict and show relationships among variables between systems and their components in the natural and designed world(s).

Continued

Table 4.3. (*continued*)

Develop a model based on evidence to illustrate the relationships between systems or between components of a system.

Constructing Explanations and Designing Solutions

Constructing explanations and designing solutions in 9–12 builds on K–8 experiences and progresses to explanations and designs that are supported by multiple and independent student-generated sources of evidence consistent with scientific ideas, principles, and theories.

Apply scientific reasoning to link evidence to the claims to assess the extent to which the reasoning and data support the explanation or conclusion.

Construct an explanation based on valid and reliable evidence obtained from a variety of sources (including students' own investigations, models, theories, simulations, peer review) and the assumption that theories and laws that describe the natural world operate today as they did in the past and will continue to do so in the future.

Engaging in Argument from Evidence

Engaging in argument from evidence in 9–12 builds on K–8 experiences and progresses to using appropriate and sufficient evidence and scientific reasoning to defend and critique claims and explanations about the natural and designed world(s). Arguments may also come from current scientific or historical episodes in science.

Construct an oral and written argument or counter-arguments based on data and evidence.

COMMON CORE MATHEMATICS STANDARDS

MATHEMATICS PRACTICES

MP1 Make sense of problems and persevere in solving them.

MP3 Construct viable arguments and critique the reasoning of others.

MP5 Use appropriate tools strategically.

MP6 Attend to precision.

MP8 Look for and express regularity in repeated reasoning.

MATHEMATICS CONTENT

HSN-Q.A.2 Define appropriate quantities for the purpose of descriptive modeling.

COMMON CORE ENGLISH LANGUAGE ARTS STANDARDS

SPEAKING AND LISTENING STANDARDS

SL.9–10.2 Integrate multiple sources of information presented in diverse media or formats (e.g., visually, quantitatively, orally) evaluating the credibility and accuracy of each source.

SL.9–10.4 Present information, findings, and supporting evidence clearly, concisely, and logically such that listeners can follow the line of reasoning and the organization, development, substance, and style are appropriate to purpose, audience, and task.

SL.9–10.5 Make strategic use of digital media (e.g., textual, graphical, audio, visual, and interactive elements) in presentations to enhance understanding of findings, reasoning, and evidence and to add interest.

SL.9–10.6 Adapt speech to a variety of contexts and tasks, demonstrating command of formal Fnglish when indicated or appropriate.

21ST CENTURY SKILLS
Global Awareness, Civic Literacy, Creativity and Innovation, Critical Thinking and Problem Solving, Communication and Collaboration, Information Literacy, Media Literacy, ICT Literacy, Flexibility and Adaptability, Initiative and Self-Direction, Social and Cross Cultural Skills, Productivity and Accountability, Leadership and Responsibility

Table 4.4. Key Vocabulary for Lesson Two

Key Vocabulary*	Definition
Weather	the state of the atmosphere at a place and time as regards heat, dryness, sunshine, wind, rain, etc.
Climate Change	a change in global or regional climate patterns, in particular a change apparent from the mid to late 20th century onwards and attributed largely to the increased levels of atmospheric carbon dioxide produced by the use of fossil fuels.
Biodiversity	the variety of life in the world or in a particular ecosystem
Ocean Acidification	the falling pH levels of the ocean (rising acidity) due to the absorption of CO_2 from the atmosphere
Anthropogenic	originating in human activity (typically refers to climate)

* Vocabulary terms are provided for both teacher and student use. Teachers may choose to introduce all or some terms to students.

TEACHER BACKGROUND INFORMATION

Teachers should understand how human activity is affecting other natural processes. The teacher should be familiar with the chemistry of the oceans and how marine life is affected by fluctuations in acidity. This lesson involves a jigsaw project in which students will work together in teams to investigate Earth's changing processes, therefore teachers should be familiar with this cooperative learning practice, which involves organizing small groups of students in "home groups" to research a component of a larger topic then share their expertise with other home groups who were assigned

other components of the larger topic. Together, all expert group members have the opportunity to share their knowledge and learn from their peers about their sub-topic. Upon completion, all students should gain a clear understanding of the larger topic and how the various sub-topics fit within it. In addition to the jigsaw strategy, the teacher should also know and understand the different political stances on climate change in preparation for any questions that students with prior knowledge of the subject might have. Teachers can navigate to the Intergovernmental Panel on Climate Change (http://ipcc.ch/) to review current scientific positions on climate change. They may then view a variety of articles published by organizations that are skeptical of climate change science. The American Enterprise Institute is perhaps the most prominent of these organizations. Articles related to climate change can be found at http://www.aei.org/?s=climate+change.

LESSON PREPARATION

During this lesson the teacher will introduce the concept of anthropogenic climate change. Each student will choose to research one of the following: biodiversity, glacial melting (sea level rise), ocean acidification, plate tectonics, or global population. Groups will split to research with other students who are investigating the same topic, then reconvene to share their findings. Additionally, students will complete an individual "If, Then" activity in which students apply their understanding of Earth's processes to further grasp the consequences of these changes.

In addition to this core lesson, an extension opportunity is suggested. If this extension is applicable, the teacher will need to collaborate with teachers from other disciplines, specifically social studies. It is recommended that the classes begin collaboration during this lesson, and continue learning together for the remainder of the unit.

LEARNING PLAN COMPONENTS
Introductory Activity/Engagement
Science Class

Connections to the Challenge: Begin each day of this lesson by directing students' attention to the driving question for the module and challenge, asking "What major geologic changes are occurring on Earth currently?" Hold a brief student discussion of how their learning in the previous days' lesson(s) contributed to their ability to create their innovation for the final challenge. You may wish to hold a class discussion, creating a class list of key ideas on chart paper or the board, or you may wish to have students create a STEM Research Notebook entry with this information.

STEM Research Notebook Prompt

Students should discuss this question as a class based on their research from the previous days. After considering this question and recording any key ideas in their STEM Research Notebooks, students should then discuss the following prompt:

How does global climate affect the natural processes on Earth?

This question will likely be more difficult for students to answer, as students have not yet discussed the relationships between climate, weather, and geological processes. The teacher should encourage students to provide any answers they feel might be appropriate, and compile responses on the board. Students should engage with one another's ideas and discuss whether ideas make sense or do not. Students should settle on a few key ways in which global climate and natural processes are related, and record these key findings in their STEM Research Notebooks.

Introduce students to the concepts of biodiversity, glacial melting (sea level rise), ocean acidifications, plate tectonics, and global population. A brief lecture on these topics should provide students with a broad definition of each of these topics, but the teacher should not go deep into detail so that students can conduct their own investigations of these topics.

Biodiversity

Teachers should explain biodiversity given the scope of the explanation below.

Biodiversity is an environment that has a great deal of different types of plants and animal species. Biodiversity can refer to a number of units of life, ranging from genes to organisms. That is, biodiversity of genetic pool is as important as biodiversity of organisms in an ecosystem.

Leave students at the definitional understanding of biodiversity and that it is important, but let them discover why it is important in their research.

Glacial melting

Teachers should explain glacial melting given the scope of the explanation below.

A glacier is a large mass of ice formed over many years. The extremely large masses of ice do not typically melt during the summer. However, glaciers have been melting at a faster rate recently and this has implications for other processes on the Earth

Leave students at the definitional understanding of glacial melting and that it is important, but let them discover why it is important in their research.

Ocean acidifications

Teachers should explain ocean acidification given the scope of the explanation below.

Oceans make up more surface area of the Earth than land, so when changes happen to the ocean, they have effects on all of the Earth. The oceans absorb about 30 percent of the carbon dioxide that is released in the atmosphere, and due to the industrial revolution, there has been more carbon dioxide in the atmosphere in recent years. When carbon dioxide is absorbed into the ocean water, chemical reactions happen that result in the increase of hydrogen ions, which make the ocean more acidic. The change in pH of the ocean has many implications for life on Earth.

Leave students at the definitional understanding of ocean acidification and that it is important, but let them discover why it is important in their research.

Plate tectonics

Teachers should explain plate tectonics given the scope of the explanation below.

Plate tectonics is the name of a theory that describes how the earth's crust changes over time through the movement of seven huge plates in the Earth's lithosphere, below the surface. The Earth acts much like potato chip continents riding on an underground sea of honey (magma). This movement continues today and is still changing the Earth's surface.

Leave students at the definitional understanding of plate tectonics and that it is important, but let them discover why it is important in their research.

Global population

Students will work in small groups to complete the jigsaw activity discussing each of these concepts. Students should get in groups of five which is also student "home groups", then within each group, students should select a research topic from one of the following: biodiversity, glacial melting (sea level rise), ocean acidification, plate tectonics, or global population. Student groups will then split again into "expert groups" so that all students who are investigating the same topic will work together to explore *the relationship between their topic and anthropogenic climate change* (i.e. all students who selected "biodiversity" should work together to discuss how biodiversity and anthropogenic climate change are related). Students should use reliable internet resources to take notes and record the explanations of each of the concepts. When the expert groups are confident that they have captured the important ideas about the relationship of their concept to anthropogenic climate change, the students go back to their home groups. Each student in the home group is an expert on a different topic, and should explain their findings to the home group. Meanwhile, students should be taking notes in their STEM Research notebooks to use later for reference in the Era of Humans Challenge.

Mathematics Connections

Students will conduct graphical and statistical interpretations of the human-influenced processes topic assigned in science class. Students should focus on their chosen research topic (i.e. if assigned to explore biodiversity, students might analyze numerical changes in biodiversity and their relationships to changes in temperatures, sea level rise, etc.). This data will become part of the information that students report back to their groups in poster or presentation format.

ELA Connections

The class will define and present the key vocabulary terms for the lesson. Encourage students to develop a concept map and/or draw pictures to present their words in an interactive format. Using the Frayer Model may also be beneficial in supporting students' vocabulary attainment. In this method, students create a graphic organizer and create a visual reference for their vocabulary words. See http://www.adlit.org/strategies/22369/ for more information about the Frayer Model. A sample Frayer Model can be found at the end of this lesson.

Social Studies Connections

Using the list of major events in human history (the origination of agriculture, the Age of European Exploration, the Industrial Revolution, the Great Acceleration, or the Information Age), students will arrange the events in chronological order and add them to the football field timeline created in Lesson One. Students will then begin compiling resources related to these periods in history to begin determining which event best marks the beginning of the Anthropocene Epoch.

ACTIVITY/INVESTIGATION
Science Class

Expert groups will investigate the chosen topic, biodiversity, glacier melting, ocean acidification, or plate tectonics, focusing on how the topic of study came to be and what the current trend is. Students should specifically focus on why scientists are interested in this phenomenon in relation to global climate change. Students should also consider why the discussion topic matters to people and to organisms. For example, the group considering sea level rise might consider, what are the implications for humans if sea levels rise? Within this expert group, students should create an artifact, such as a poster or electronic presentation, to share information with their home groups. All students within the expert groups should feel comfortable presenting the information

that the group compiles, as the students will return to their original groups and must serve as "experts" in their topic of discussion.

Mathematics Connections

Students will work in their expert groups to find relevant data about each of the phenomena, biodiversity, glacier melting, ocean acidification, and plate tectonics, and create an infographic of the data to explain the phenomena quantitatively to the home groups. Infographics are posters that are stylized visualizations to clearly explain the quantitative trends in a topic. There are several free infographic templates found at:

Canva – www.canva.com

Easelly – www.easel.ly/create/

Piktochart – https://piktochart.com

There may be a registration involved to use the software. Alternatively students can create science-fair type boards that explain the quantitative trends that students found regarding their expert topic.

When infographics/posters are completed, students should do a gallery walk to evaluate all of the posters to ensure appropriate measures and presentation thereof (e.g. using mean temperatures). Students should critique data and graphs used.

Conduct a brief discussion about the ethics of presenting data in a way that does not misrepresent information. Some examples are not including values on one of the axes; skewing y-axis values to make them look smaller or bigger, representing percentages without starting at zero (which makes the smaller percentages look smaller).

ELA Connections

ELA students can support or challenge the variety of perspectives on climate change by reviewing the Intergovernmental Panel on Climate Change (http://ipcc.ch/) website to review current scientific positions on climate change. They may then view a variety of articles published by organizations that are skeptical of climate change science. The American Enterprise Institute is perhaps the most prominent of these organizations. Articles from this organization related to climate change can be found at http://www.aei.org/?s=climate+change. Students can use the following chart to compare and contrast the ideas presented in the two different positions on climate change.

Climate change arguments

Topic	Intergovernmental Panel on Climate Change position	American Enterprise Institute position
Global warming	Warming of the climate system is unequivocal, and since the 1950s, many of the observed changes are unprecedented over decades to millennia	Few people feel particularly strongly about global warming
	Each of the last three decades has been successively warmer at the Earth's surface than any preceding decade since 1850	A majority of Americans now believe the effects of global warming have already begun and that global warming is caused by human activities, but most still do not think it will pose a serious threat to them within their lifetime.
Ocean changes	Ocean warming dominates the increase in energy stored in the climate system, accounting for more than 90% of the energy accumulated between 1971 and 2010	Carbon dioxide at a 20-year low according to an editorial in Investor's Business Daily

Note to students that the IPCC uses data collected from nature and the AEI uses opinions to make their point. Conduct a whole class discussion about the sources of information and what science relies upon for knowledge building.

Social Studies Connections

Students will examine the resources compiled for each topic in the comparison chart above, to ensure attention to tenets of historical thinking including credibility of evidence, and attention to multiple perspectives. Have students individually note in their STEM Research Notebook about the following questions.

Where and when was this resource disseminated?

Who is the author of this resource?

What are their credentials to report on scientific phenomena?

Who is the intended audience?

Conduct a whole class discussion making an argument for positions on climate change based on scientific evidence. Students should evaluate the claims, evidence,

and reasoning they use in their verbal argument for their position. Students should use a rubric to help them guide a civil and logical discussion. The rubric is found at the end of this lesson.

EXPLAIN
Science Class

Students will reconvene in their original groups and share each expert artifact. The group will discuss how anthropogenic climate change has affected the globe and the severity of these changing processes. Students should record key findings from the groups in their STEM Research Notebooks in order to reference this information later. Students will be assessed on their contributions according to the rubric at the end of lesson two.

Mathematics Connections

Students will use data collected in science and use appropriate methods to present data (i.e. students should know when to use line graphs, pie charts, etc.). Students should present data in their posters and presentations in appropriate ways, paying attention to ethical data reporting issues.

ELA Connections

Students can assemble data exploring the five main concepts students learned about in science class, and use that data to assess the validity of each side of the climate change debate. Students may then engage in a debate, orally presenting evidence and defending a specific position. Students must use data to defend their positions.

Social Studies Connections

Students will annotate resources found to describe each of the time periods. Teachers might want to use the following lesson to help students find meaningful and useful ways to annotate texts: http://learning.blogs.nytimes.com/2011/03/07/briefly-noted-practicing-useful-annotation-strategies/.

EXTEND/APPLY KNOWLEDGE
Science Class

Students will continue the jigsaw activity as needed in order to fully explore the ways in which anthropogenic climate change is related to biodiversity, glacial melt, etc. Once students are confident in their understandings of the five main concepts, teachers will challenge students to complete "If, Then" statements based on their knowledge of these variables. Using the "If, Then" format (provided at the end of the lesson), students will individually hypothesize on potential combined effects of the changing processes on Earth. The teacher should walk through an example "If, Then" activity with students, then should allow students to individually develop three more of these statements. Students should complete this activity individually in order for the teacher to assess student knowledge of interactions between the earth and these variables. Students should each turn in three "If, Then" statements for teacher evaluation.

Mathematics Connections

Students find numerical data to support their "If, Then" statement. This will likely include data from the past century focused on any of the assigned topics (biodiversity, glacial melting (sea level rise), ocean acidification, plate tectonics, or global population).

ELA Connections

Students will develop a persuasive essay on climate change that uses data collected from their research. Students are also welcome to incorporate talking points learned through the debate activity that took place in previous days. Students should be sure to properly cite data to back up their claims.

Social Studies Connections

Students will create a resource kit for future research that compiles the information about the periods that may mark the beginning the Anthropocene Epoch.

The resource kit will include individual pages for each of the resources. The information recorded on each of these pages includes

- Major topic addressed

- Citation of the resource

- Key points in the article

- Example of how to communicate this information in the multimedia presentation The Era of Humans Challenge

A chart to help organize this information is included at the end of this lesson.

EVALUATE/ASSESSMENT
Performance Tasks

Expert group presentations on global processes in the form of expert group posters presented and displayed around the classroom for the remainder of the unit for student reference.

If, then assignment (see attached worksheet)

INTERNET RESOURCES

http://www.adlit.org/strategies/22371/ This website offers an overview and teaching ideas related to jigsaw strategies.

http://ipcc.ch/ The website for the Intergovernmental Panel on Climate Change. This site brings together current research and policy on this topic from an international perspective.

http://www.aei.org/?s=climate+change A series of articles and resources from The American Enterprise Institute.

http://www.globalissues.org/article/171/loss-of-biodiversity-and-extinctions# MassiveExtinctionsFromHumanActivity A multimedia article focused on global climate and health issues with many related links. This link also provides detailed references and information regarding resource verification. As such, it is also useful for students to practice ways to verify credibility in online resources.

http://ocean.si.edu/ocean-acidification An informative overview from the Smithsonian Museum of Natural History of ocean acidification and why it matters

http://www.adlit.org/strategies/22369/ This site will be useful for teachers unfamiliar with the Frayer Model for vocabulary building.

http://learning.blogs.nytimes.com/2011/03/07/briefly-noted-practicing-useful-annotation-strategies/ A lesson plan that helps students learn to annotate texts in useful ways.

Name:_____Date:_____

If, Then . . .

Based on your research of global processes, use the following format to describe the consequences of a single change due to anthropogenics (e.g. increase in global population, global temperature rise, ocean acidification), and then describe the cumulative effects of multiple changes to Earth's processes.

If _____ is changed by . . .
(manipulated variable)

then _____ will . . .
(responding variable)

because . . .

Jigsaw Rubric

	Expert	Competent	Emerging	Does Not Meet Expectations	Score
Participation and Presentation	Student used time well focusing attention on the task. Appropriate communication (e.g. appropriate voice volume) was used throughout.	Student mostly used time well and stayed focused on the task, but student failed to adhere to appropriate communication expectations	Student lost focus on task at least once or failed to adhere to appropriate communication expectations	Student lost focus more than once, or failed on more than once occasion to use modest voice volume, or student was uncooperative about participating.	
Content	*All* information given was accurate and detailed. Information presented in an easy to understand manner.	*Most* information given was accurate and detailed in an easy to understand	Information given was lacking key information.	Information given was lacking key information and difficult to understand.	
Impact on Living Things	Student has a clear understanding of the impact of the issue on human civilization and other living organisms.	Student explores some of the reasons why their topic is important to humans and other living organisms.	Student explores some of the reasons why their topic is important to humans, but not to other life, or v/v.	Student provides little (if any warrant) for exploring this topic and its relation to living things.	
Graphics	Graphic representation was neat and directly pertinent to content.	Graphic representation was neat and easy to understand.	Graphic representation was either messy or hard to understand.	Graphic representation was messy and hard to understand.	

Figure 4.1. Frayer Model Graphic Organizer

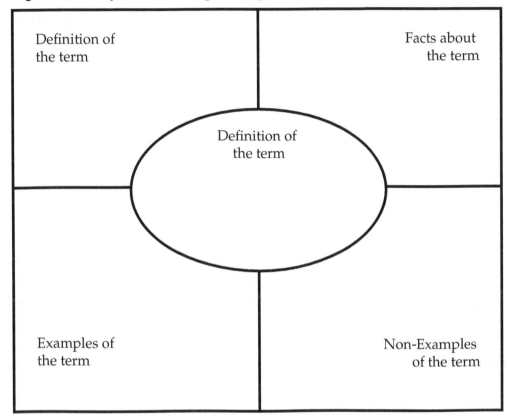

Rubric for Verbal Argumentation (whole class or small group)

Characteristic	Emerging (1)	Proficient (2)	Exemplary (3)
Follows guidelines of intellectual discussion and is civil	Criticizes other people personally instead of being critical of ideas; doesn't use appropriate language	Challenges the idea but without reason; uses appropriate language	Challenges the idea with solid reasoning; uses appropriate language; diverts any unproductive discussion
Makes claim	Claim unoriginal AND indirectly related to topic	Claim original AND indirectly related to topic	Claim original AND directly related to topic
Uses reliable sources for evidence	Uses unreliable resources (such as Wikipedia or blog)	Only uses textbook as resource	Uses outside reliable resources (such as a scientific journal or .gov or .edu website)
Appropriate level of evidence	Opinion-based evidence	One piece of researched evidence	More than one piece of researched evidence
Responds to the content of the discussion	No response or unrelated to claim	Response is indirectly associated with claim	Response is aligned with claim
Connects with what prior person says	Unrelated to current discussion	Stays on topic, but makes no connection with person before them	Acknowledges prior person's idea and elaborates on what previous person says
Able to defend their claim/rebuttal	Has no response	Has a response but cannot back up response	Has a response and is able to back up response with further evidence
Uses appropriate reasoning	Reasoning is disconnected from claim	Reasoning is superficially connected to claim	Reasoning directly connects claim to evidence

NATIONAL SCIENCE TEACHING ASSOCIATION

RESOURCE KIT for ERA of HUMANS CHALLENGE	Page # _____
Major topic addressed	
Citation of the resource	
How is this a scientifically reliable resource?	
Key points in the article	
Example of how to communicate this information in the multimedia presentation The Era of Humans Challenge	

Lesson Plan 3
The Anthropocene: Exploring and Deliberating a New Epoch in Geologic Time

LESSON THREE SUMMARY

In this lesson, students will use the information they have gathered on Earth's processes in Lesson two, and how boundaries of an era are defined in lesson one to synthesize their data, identify geologically significant moments in human history and propose a specific event or time period to serve as the boundary between the Holocene and the Anthropocene. The first days of this lesson include information sharing between history and science to gain a collective understanding of the nature of science and historical thinking as well as specific applications of these ways of knowing. History students, for example, will provide annotated resources pertaining to the potential Anthropocene epoch boundary while science students will share information about Earth's formation and human-induced phenomena. Together, they will develop and present their multi-media boundary proposition as a consultation team to a publisher. Teachers might consider inviting a school administrator or community member to serve in this role during presentations. Finally, individual students will develop textbook entries for these publishers.

ESSENTIAL QUESTION(S)

Which human developments most clearly affected the way the Earth works today? How can these events be determined in the geologic record? What are the defining factors of the Holocene and what is different about the Anthropocene?

ESTABLISHED GOALS/OBJECTIVES

At the conclusion of this lesson, students will be able to:

- collaborate with a team to determine geologically significant human events;

- comprehend the critical differences between the Holocene and proposed Anthropocene epochs;

- develop a comprehensive report proposing supporting evidence for a single time period for the boundary event between the Holocene and Anthropocene epochs

TIME REQUIRED

13 days (approximately 45 minutes each; Days 12–24 in the schedule). During Days 17–19 students will largely focus on the development of their consulting presentation

to the textbook publishers. During Days 20–21, groups will present and the class will have a debriefing. The final three days will be for individual students to develop their textbook entries, including the text (2–3 paragraphs) with at least three related images, graphs, or figures.

NECESSARY MATERIALS

Internet access and access to PowerPoint or other presentation software.

Table 4.5. Standards Addressed in STEM Road Map Module Lesson Three

---

NEXT GENERATION SCIENCE STANDARDS

PERFORMANCE EXPECTATIONS

HS-LS2–1 Use mathematical and/or computational representations to support explanations of factors that affect carrying capacity of ecosystems at different scales.

HS-LS2–2 Use mathematical representations to support and revise explanations based on evidence about factors affecting biodiversity and populations in ecosystems of different scales.

HS-ESS1–6 Apply scientific reasoning and evidence from ancient Earth materials, meteorites, and other planetary surfaces to construct an account of Earth's formation and early history.

HS-ESS2–1 Develop a model to illustrate how Earth's internal and surface processes operate at different spatial and temporal scales to form continental and ocean-floor features.

HS-ESS2–2 Analyze geoscience data to make the claim that one change to Earth's surface can create feedbacks that cause changes to other Earth systems.

HS-ESS2–7 Construct an argument based on evidence about the simultaneous coevolution of Earth's systems and life on Earth.

HS-ESS3–1 Construct an explanation based on evidence for how the availability of natural, occurrence of natural hazards, and changes in climate have influenced human activity.

DISCIPLINARY CORE IDEAS

LS2.A: Interdependent Relationships in Ecosystems

Ecosystems have carrying capacities, which are limits to the numbers of organisms and populations they can support. These limits result from such factors as the availability of living and nonliving resources and from such challenges such as predation, competition, and disease. Organisms would have the capacity to produce populations of great size were it not for the fact that environments and resources are finite. This fundamental tension affects the abundance (number of individuals) of species in any given ecosystem.

Continued

Table 4.5. (*continued*)

LS2.C: Ecosystem Dynamics, Functioning, and Resilience

A complex set of interactions within an ecosystem can keep its numbers and types of organisms relatively constant over long periods of time under stable conditions. If a modest biological or physical disturbance to an ecosystem occurs, it may return to its more or less original status (i.e., the ecosystem is resilient), as opposed to becoming a very different ecosystem. Extreme fluctuations in conditions or the size of any population, however, can challenge the functioning of ecosystems in terms of resources and habitat availability.

ESS1.C: The History of Planet Earth

Although active geologic processes, such as plate tectonics and erosion, have destroyed or altered most of the very early rock record on Earth, other objects in the solar system, such as lunar rocks, asteroids, and meteorites, have changed little over billions of years. Studying these objects can provide information about Earth's formation and early history.

ESS2.A: Earth Materials and Systems

Earth's systems, being dynamic and interacting, cause feedback effects that can increase or decrease the original changes.

ESS2.B: Plate Tectonics and Large-Scale System Interactions

Plate tectonics is the unifying theory that explains the past and current movements of the rocks at Earth's surface and provides a framework for understanding its geologic history. Plate movements are responsible for most continental and ocean-floor features and for the distribution of most rocks and minerals within Earth's crust. (ESS2.B Grade 8 GBE)

ESS2.D: Weather and Climate

The foundation for Earth's global climate systems is the electromagnetic radiation from the sun, as well as its reflection, absorption, storage, and redistribution among the atmosphere, ocean, and land systems, and this energy's re-radiation into space.

ESS2.E Biogeology

The many dynamic and delicate feedbacks between the biosphere and other Earth systems cause a continual co-evolution of Earth's surface and the life that exists on it.

ESS3.A: Natural Resources

Resource availability has guided the development of human society.

ESS3.B: Natural Hazards

Natural hazards and other geologic events have shaped the course of human history; [they] have significantly altered the sizes of human populations and have driven human migrations.

PS1.C: Nuclear Processes

Spontaneous radioactive decays follow a characteristic exponential decay law. Nuclear lifetimes allow radiometric dating to be used to determine the ages of rocks and other materials. (secondary)

CROSSCUTTING CONCEPTS

Scale, Proportion, and Quantity

The significance of a phenomenon is dependent on the scale, proportion, and quantity at which it occurs.

Scale, Proportion, and Quantity

Using the concept of orders of magnitude allows one to understand how a model at one scale relates to a model at another scale.

Stability and Change

Much of science deals with constructing explanations of how things change and how they remain stable.

Cause and Effect

Empirical evidence is required to differentiate between cause and correlation and make claims about specific causes and effects.

Connections to Nature of Science

Scientific Knowledge is Open to Revision in Light of New Evidence

Most scientific knowledge is quite durable, but is, in principle, subject to change based on new evidence and/or reinterpretation of existing evidence.

Science Models, Laws, Mechanisms, and Theories Explain Natural Phenomena

A scientific theory is a substantiated explanation of some aspect of the natural world, based on a body of facts that have been repeatedly confirmed through observation and experiment and the science community validates each theory before it is accepted. If new evidence is discovered that the theory does not accommodate, the theory is generally modified in light of this new evidence.

Models, mechanisms, and explanations collectively serve as tools in the development of a scientific theory

Connections to Engineering, Technology, and Applications of Science

Influence of Science, Engineering, and Technology on Society and the Natural World

Modern civilization depends on major technological systems.

SCIENCE AND ENGINEERING PRACTICES

Using Mathematics and Computational Thinking

Mathematical and computational thinking in 9–12 builds on K-8 experiences and progresses to using algebraic thinking and analysis, a range of linear and nonlinear functions including trigonometric functions, exponentials and logarithms, and computational tools for statistical analysis to analyze, represent, and model data. Simple computational simulations are created and used based on mathematical models of basic assumptions.

Use mathematical and/or computational representations of phenomena or design solutions to support explanations.

Continued

Table 4.5. (*continued*)

Developing and Using Models

Modeling in 9–12 builds on K–8 experiences and progresses to using, synthesizing, and developing models to predict and show relationships among variables between systems and their components in the natural and designed world(s).

Develop a model based on evidence to illustrate the relationships between systems or between components of a system.

Constructing Explanations and Designing Solutions

Constructing explanations and designing solutions in 9–12 builds on K–8 experiences and progresses to explanations and designs that are supported by multiple and independent student-generated sources of evidence consistent with scientific ideas, principles, and theories.

Apply scientific reasoning to link evidence to the claims to assess the extent to which the reasoning and data support the explanation or conclusion.

Construct an explanation based on valid and reliable evidence obtained from a variety of sources (including students' own investigations, models, theories, simulations, peer review) and the assumption that theories and laws that describe the natural world operate today as they did in the past and will continue to do so in the future.

Analyzing and Interpreting Data

Analyzing data in 9–12 builds on K–8 experiences and progresses to introducing more detailed statistical analysis, the comparison of data sets for consistency, and the use of models to generate and analyze data.

Analyze data using tools, technologies, and/or models (e.g., computational, mathematical) in order to make valid and reliable scientific claims or determine an optimal design solution.

Engaging in Argument from Evidence

Engaging in argument from evidence in 9–12 builds on K–8 experiences and progresses to using appropriate and sufficient evidence and scientific reasoning to defend and critique claims and explanations about the natural and designed world(s). Arguments may also come from current scientific or historical episodes in science.

Construct an oral and written argument or counter-arguments based on data and evidence.

COMMON CORE MATHEMATICS STANDARDS

MATHEMATICS PRACTICES

MP1 Make sense of problems and persevere in solving them.

MP3 Construct viable arguments and critique the reasoning of others.

MP5 Use appropriate tools strategically.

MP6 Attend to precision.

MP8 Look for and express regularity in repeated reasoning.

Mathematics Content

HSN. RN.A.1 Explain how the definition of the meaning of rational exponents follows from extending the properties of integer exponents to those values, allowing for a notation for radicals in terms of rational exponents.

HSN.Q.A.1 Use units as a way to understand problems and to guide the solution of multi-step problems; choose and interpret units consistently in formulas; choose and interpret the scale and the origin in graphs and data displays.

HSN-Q.A.2 Define appropriate quantities for the purpose of descriptive modeling.

HSS-ID.A.1 Represent data with plots on the real number line.

COMMON CORE ENGLISH/LANGUAGE ARTS STANDARDS
READING STANDARDS

RI.9–10.1 Cite strong and thorough textual evidence to support analysis of what the text says explicitly as well as inferences drawn from the text.

RI.9–10.2 Determine a central idea of a text and analyze its development over the course of the text, including how it emerges and is shaped and refined by specific details; provide an objective summary of the text.

RI.9–10.7 Analyze various accounts of a subject told in different mediums (e.g., a person's life story in both print and multimedia), determining which details are emphasized in each account.

RI.9–10.8 Delineate and evaluate the argument and specific claims in a text, assessing whether the reasoning is valid and the evidence is relevant and sufficient; identify false statements and fallacious reasoning.

RI.9–10.10 By the end of grade 9, read and comprehend literacy nonfiction in the grades 9–10 text complexity band proficiently, with scaffolding as needed at the high end of the range.

WRITING STANDARDS

W.9–10.1a Introduce precise claim(s), distinguish the claim(s) from alternate or opposing claims, and create an organization that establishes clear relationships among claim(s), counterclaims, reasons, and evidence.

W.9–10.1b Develop claim(s) and counterclaims fairly, supplying evidence for each while pointing out the strengths and limitations of both in a manner that anticipates the audience's knowledge level and concerns.

W.9–10.1c Use words, phrases, and clauses to link the major sections of the text, create cohesion, and clarify the relationships between claim(s) and reasons, between reasons and evidence, and between claim(s) and counterclaims.

W.9–10.1d Establish and maintain a formal style and objective tone while attending to the norms and conventions of the discipline in which they are writing.

W.9–10.1e Provide a concluding statement or section that follows from and supports the argument presented.

Continued

Table 4.5. (*continued*)

W.9–10.2a Introduce a topic; organize complex ideas, concepts, and information to make important connections and distinctions; include formatting (e.g., headings), graphics (e.g., figures, tables), and multimedia when useful to aiding comprehension.

W.9–10.2b Develop the topic with well-chosen, relevant, and sufficient facts, extended definitions, concrete details, quotations, or other information and examples appropriate to the audience's knowledge of the topic.

W.9–10.2c Use appropriate and varied transitions to link the major sections of the text, create cohesion, and clarify the relationships among complex ideas and concepts.

W.9–10.2d Use precise language and domain-specific vocabulary to manage the complexity of the topic.

W.9–10.2e Establish and maintain a formal style and objective tone while attending to the norms and conventions of the discipline in which they are writing.

W.9–10.2f Provide a concluding statement or section that follows from and supports the information or explanation presented (e.g., articulating implications or the significance of the topic).

W.9–10.4 Produce clear and coherent writing in which the development, organization, and style are appropriate to task, purpose, and audience.

W.9–10.6 Use technology, including the Internet, to produce, publish, and update individual or shared writing products, taking advantage of technology's capacity to link to other information and to display information flexibly and dynamically.

W.9–10.8 Gather relevant information from multiple authoritative print and digital sources, using advanced searches effectively; assess the usefulness of each source in answering the research question; integrate information into the text selectively to maintain the flow of ideas, avoiding plagiarism and following a standard format for citation.

W.9–10.10 Write routinely over extended time frames (time for research, reflection, and revision) and shorter time frames (a single sitting or a day or two) for a range of tasks, purposes, and audiences.

SPEAKING AND LISTENING STANDARDS

SL.9–10.1 Initiate and participate effectively in a range of collaborative discussions (one-on-one, in groups, and teacher-led) with diverse partners on grades 9–10 topics, texts, and issues, building on others' ideas and expressing their own clearly and persuasively.

SL.9–10.2 Integrate multiple sources of information presented in diverse media or formats (e.g., visually, quantitatively, orally) evaluating the credibility and accuracy of each source.

SL.9–10.4 Present information, findings, and supporting evidence clearly, concisely, and logically such that listeners can follow the line of reasoning and the organization, development, substance, and style are appropriate to purpose, audience, and task.

SL.9–10.5 Make strategic use of digital media (e.g., textual, graphical, audio, visual, and interactive elements) in presentations to enhance understanding of findings, reasoning, and evidence and to add interest.

SL.9–10.6 Adapt speech to a variety of contexts and tasks, demonstrating command of formal English when indicated or appropriate.

Table 4.6. Key Vocabulary in Lesson Three

Key Vocabulary*	Definition
Agriculture	The cultivation of plants and animals to provide food and sustenance for human life.
Age Of Exploration	A period between approximately 1400–1700 CE during which Europeans navigated the planet in search of discovery, resources, wealth, and colonial power.
Industrial Revolution	The transition to new processes of manufacturing that began in Western Europe and occurred between the mid-eighteenth and early twentieth centuries. This period is characterized by economic growth, innovation in manufacturing and transportation, and rise in urbanization as well as income inequality, pollution, and the degradation of natural resources.
Great Acceleration	Historians argue that the period known as the Great Acceleration began as an outgrowth of the Industrial Revolution. In this period, which arguably began in the late nineteenth century and continued through the twentieth century, we see rapid growth in negative effects of industrialization including rainforest depletion, ocean acidification, and ozone layer degradation.
Information Age	This term is used to describe the age of humankind in which computer technology and the Internet has permeated humanity. In the Information Age, we see a transition from traditional industry to a knowledge-based globalized economy where efficiency, innovation, and rapid global networking communications drive societies.

* Vocabulary terms are provided for both teacher and student use. Teachers may choose to introduce all or some terms to students.

TEACHER BACKGROUND INFORMATION

This lesson focuses mainly on human history and the results of modern civilization, and is an excellent continuation of the extension opportunity from Lesson Two. Collaborating teachers should guide students towards noteworthy periods in human history to determine which had the most significant effect on the planet. The students should explore these periods and develop a thesis with supporting facts for which suggested period, or one of their own, should serve as the boundary event between the Holocene and Anthropocene. The students will construct a presentation to submit their boundary event suggestion to a team of textbook writers who are considering adding the Anthropocene to the latest edition of a geology textbook. The students will need to be professional and persuasive in their proposals.

One challenging presentation format is Pecha Kucha (see http://www.pechaku cha.org for more information). Briefly, this format is designed to maximize audience engagement and avoid typical pitfalls of long, pedantic presentations by providing a format in which 20 images are each shown for 20 seconds with the narrator talking as the images scroll. Additionally, the TED (Technology, Entertainment, Design) blog offers a great post about developing presentation slides that help presenters communicate their ideas effectively (see http://blog.ted.com/10-tips-for-better-slide-decks/). Although not specifically aligned to Pecha Kucha, the ideas work in concert.

The final three days will be for individual students to develop a sample textbook entry. This assignment should include the text (2–3 paragraphs) with at least three related images, graphs, or figures. These may be some used in the presentation to textbook publishers.

LESSON PREPARATION

Preparation for the activities in this lesson involves establishing expectations for the textbook excerpt and the final presentation. Providing students examples of formats for these two summative artifacts will allow teams to develop creative and informative ways to share the information they have analyzed.

LEARNING PLAN COMPONENTS
Introductory Activity/Engagement

Days 12–15

Science Class

Connections to the Challenge: Begin each day of this lesson by directing students' attention to the driving question for the module and challenge.

STEM Research Notebook Prompt

Ask students to respond to the following thought-provoking question,

Which period in human history most clearly affected the way the Earth works today?
Students should reflect on their responses to this question which were developed on Day 10 of the module, and should be recorded in their STEM Research Notebooks. In documentary groups, students should discuss how their learning in the previous days' lessons contributed to their ability to create their innovation for the final challenge (as outlined in the Lesson Preparation section). You may wish to hold a class discussion, creating a class list of key ideas on chart paper or the board, or you may wish to have students create a STEM Research Notebook entry with this information. Students will review science notebooks and artifacts created and hold a discussion about the most important ideas they learned about healthy living at the cellular level. Students can complete the reasoning chain discussion frame "I used to think . . . but now I think . . . because . . ." Students should first record these ideas in their STEM Research Notebooks and then share them with the class.

STEM Research Notebook Prompt

The teacher should direct students to focus on the following thought-provoking question:

How can these events be determined in the geologic record?
Students should think about this with a partner or in groups of three and then share out their ideas to the class. Students should engage with one another's answers, pushing students to think more deeply about their responses. The teacher should record key notes on the board, then students should record these key ideas in their STEM Research Notebooks. Teachers should then challenge students to consider the following question:

How can these events be determined in the geologic record?
Students should consider how humans have impacted landscapes and the types of materials future scientists might find to talk about this period in geologic history. Students should record key thoughts from this discussion in their STEM Research Notebooks.

Review Earth science textbook entries. Discuss quality of the arguments, readability, and intended audience. Teachers are encouraged to bring textbooks from many different time periods in for students to analyze. Focus students on looking at the language and image choices and content clarity authors use to share information. Students should record ideas for their own textbook submissions in their STEM Research Notebooks in order to reference these notes when they construct their own textbook sections.

The teacher should then lead students in thinking about the "nature of science," or the elements that guide scientific research and knowledge generation. Depending on

time available, teachers are encouraged to use nature of science activities to engage students in thinking about the nature of science, rather than lecture. Nature of science lesson plans can be found here: http://www.indiana.edu/~ensiweb/natsc.fs.html

Students should specifically consider the practices scientists might use tools and research techniques to approach questions related to geologic changes and climate change. Students should work in groups of three to four to investigate a main way in which scientists might research climate change. Students and teachers might reference the following websites in order to understand the work of researchers engaged in the study of climate change:

http://know.climateofconcern.org/index.php?option=com_content&task=article&id=71 – A broad overview of four main methods used by climate scientists to understand climate change

https://www.ncas.ac.uk/index.php/en/how-do-ncas-scientists-study-climate A broad overview of the ways in which scientific knowledge on climate change is analyzed then disseminated to the public

https://www.ncdc.noaa.gov/news/how-do-scientists-study-ancient-climates A quick overview of the ways in which scientists study climate change

http://www.smithsonianmag.com/science-nature/five-unusual-ways-scientists-are-studying-climate-change-1308349/?no-ist – Unique ways that scientists are studying climate change

https://www.climate.gov/news-features/climate-tech/climate-core-how-scientists-study-ice-cores-reveal-earth%E2%80%99s-climate – How ice cores are used to study climate change

http://climate.nasa.gov/ NASA's website on climate change, including current data on climate change.

In groups, students should generate presentations on one way in which climate scientists research climate change. These presentations will then be given to the science class and to the history class so that students can understand different ways in which climate scientists and historians might approach research problems. Presentations will be assessed according to the rubric at the end of lesson three.

Teachers should also emphasize the collaborative nature of science, making sure students understand that researchers communicate their findings to the research community so that other researchers are aware of their findings. These researchers can then build off of multiple types of evidence in order to make their claims. Students should consider how collaborating with historians will make their research stronger.

Following student presentations from science and history classes, students should use their knowledge from the previous lessons and these presentations to collaboratively discuss where the Anthropocene might begin. Key discussion points should be recorded in the students' STEM Research Notebooks, and used when completing the graphic organizer on page 56.

Mathematics Connections

Create infographics to enhance the textbook entries they are critiquing in science class. The following website contains ideas, templates, and tutorials in creating infographics (see https://infogr.am/). <u>Students should again consider how to ethically present data and also how to present data in a clear, convincing manner.</u>

ELA Connections

Review Pecha Kucha presentation guidelines and examples. Discuss the format of the presentation and what content would be considered critical to present in such a short period of time. Students should consider what kinds of images best match the information they are presenting. Additionally, review the TED blog guidelines for quality presentations.

Social Studies Connections

Research recent textbook debates in the news (e.g. http://www.washingtonpost.com/wp-dyn/content/article/2010/03/17/AR2010031700560.html). Students should consider why different groups want to have a voice in textbook design, and consider the agendas of various groups.

Similar to the work in science class, students should then generate presentations on the ways in which historians conduct their studies. Students should present their findings to the history class as well as the social studies class, and students should compare and contrast the ways in which historians and climate scientists tackle research questions. Student presentations should be evaluated according to the rubric at the end of Lesson Three. Teachers and students could consult the following site to help them in their research: http://www.history.ac.uk/ihr/Focus/Whatishistory/marwick1.html An overview of why and how historians study history.

ACTIVITY/INVESTIGATION
Science Class

Students complete the graphic organizer (included at the end of this lesson) to help them design and develop Pecha Kucha-style presentation highlighting their understanding of criteria for boundary events. Students should use whatever resources are available (books, internet, local resources, etc.) in order to develop the most informed

claim possible. Students should consider what they learned from the research in history class, along with what they learned in science class, to define what they believe might be the beginning of the Anthropocene.

Student presentations should be developed according to the rubric found at the end of Lesson Three. Students should remember that this presentation should be given as a persuasive presentation, like one that would be given to a textbook publisher in order to convince them to include this content in the text. Students should also be reminded that the content of their presentations will also need to be converted into a textbook chapter, so they should consider how their presentations could be modified to fit a text and graphic format.

Students should use the Engineering Design Process (EDP) to create the presentation. Introduce the EDP to students as a process by which engineers and other STEM professionals solve problems and accomplish complex tasks. Emphasize to students that engineers routinely work collaboratively and that they will work as teams to solve their final challenge. The EDP will provide a framework for this group work. Show students the EDP graphic (attached at the end of this lesson) and review each of the steps with students. As they plan and create their models, they should note their progress in their STEM Research Notebooks by creating an entry for each stage of the EDP for the development of the description of the simulation.

Students should provide evidence of their use of the EDP in their STEM Research Notebooks, labeling a page with each step of the EDP and providing information appropriate to that step. You may wish to provide students with a general outline for organizing this information in their notebooks. For example:

1. Define

   a. Identify your group's target audience

   b. What is the goal of your presentation (for example, the goal might be to provide information to your audience, to persuade them of something, to clarify understandings of eras, etc.)

   c. What products do you need to produce?

2. Learn

   a. What additional information do you need?

   b. What did you find out from your research? Remember to provide citations for your information.

   c. What ideas do team members have?

3. Plan

   a. How will you schedule your work to ensure that you complete it on time?

   b. How will you divide tasks? Hint: you might want to create a chart assigning team members jobs

   c. What will your presentation be? Make a sketch or a storyboard of your multi-media presentation!

   d. What materials do you need?

4. Try

   a. Create the components of your response

      i. Goal of presentation

      ii. Written description of presentation

      iii. Storyboard of multi-media portion of presentation

5. Test

   a. Practice your presentation and get feedback from others if possible – make sure that your audience understands your goal!

   b. What worked well?

   c. What didn't work well?

6. Decide

   a. Based upon your test run(s) of your presentation, what will you change?

7. Share

   a. Share your presentations in a whole class – make sure you know who will present various parts of your presentation

Mathematics Connections

Create different data displays including infographics for Pecha Kucha presentation and textbook entry. Students should consider how infographics will look when displayed for only a short period of time (like in the presentations) and how data might be displayed when the reader might have more time to explore it (like in a textbook).

ELA Connections

Work to revise and edit presentation for readability and adherence to time and format expectations. Students should also be sure that the presentations adhere to a persuasive format.

Social Studies Connections

Add social studies elements to infographics. This should include very brief writings on sociocultural and economic impacts of human activity related to each group's decision on the event chosen as boundary for the Anthropocene Epoch. The writing here aligns with that which will be included in the textbook excerpt, but is far more concise and pointed to maintain the aesthetic of the infographic to be used in the textbook entry.

EXPLAIN
Science Class, Mathematics, ELA and Social Studies Connections

Students should present the final proposition for the historical marker for the beginning of the Anthropocene to textbook publisher. See presentation rubric at the end of this lesson.

EXTEND/APPLY KNOWLEDGE
Science Class and Social Studies Connections

Complete and submit sample textbook entry including 2–3 paragraphs of text and a minimum of three figures, images, or graphs to complement the text. A complete assessment rubric for the textbook chapter is included at the end of this lesson, and students should follow all rubric guidelines. Textbook entries should have a brief but interesting introduction, should contain references to data and/or outside resources to support claims, and should be logical and easy to read. Students should also be sure to include graphics wherever relevant.

Mathematics and ELA Connections

Review textbook entries before submission for literary and graphical accuracy. Students should particularly note flow of ideas, grammatical issues, presentation of data, and data labeling before submitting this.

EVALUATE/ASSESSMENT
PERFORMANCE TASKS

"Nature of science" presentations on climate change research

Nature of history presentations on historical research

Presentation to Publishers

Textbook Entry

Attached are resources to support the teacher in guiding and assessing student outcomes on the performance tasks

INTERNET RESOURCES

http://www.pechakucha.org This site offers explanation and examples of the Japanese presentation model of Pecha Kucha.

https://infogr.am/ This site is one of many that offer free access to developing infographics.

http://www.washingtonpost.com/wp-dyn/content/article/2010/03/17/AR 2010031700560.html This Washington Post article provides details regarding the 2010 textbook controversy in Texas. It may be a useful resource for social studies students investigating times when textbook passages made headlines.

http://www.indiana.edu/~ensiweb/natsc.fs.html A site with lesson plan ideas for teaching the "Nature of Science."

http://know.climateofconcern.org/index.php?option=com_content&task= article&id=71 – A broad overview of four main methods used by climate scientists to understand climate change.

https://www.ncas.ac.uk/index.php/en/how-do-ncas-scientists-study-climate A broad overview of the ways in which scientific knowledge on climate change is analyzed then disseminated to the public.

https://www.ncdc.noaa.gov/news/how-do-scientists-study-ancient-climates A quick overview of the ways in which scientists study climate change.

http://www.smithsonianmag.com/science-nature/five-unusual-ways-scientists-are-studying-climate-change-1308349/?no-ist Unique ways that scientists are studying climate change.

https://www.climate.gov/news-features/climate-tech/climate-core-how-scientists-study-ice-cores-reveal-earth%E2%80%99s-climate How ice cores are used to study climate change.

http://climate.nasa.gov/ NASA's website on climate change, including current data on climate change.

Web Resources for proposed boundary events

- Birth of Agriculture: A relatively brief and accessible article in Science Magazine (http://www.sciencemag.org/content/282/5393/1446.full).

- The Age of Exploration: This 30-minute YouTube video provides a nice overview of the Age of Exploration (https://www.youtube.com/watch?v=VVD6f20OG9w).

- A History Channel infographic on details about the Age of Exploration (http://www.history.com/shows/mankind-the-story-of-all-of-us/infographics/age-of-exploration).

- The Industrial Revolution: The Yale/New Haven Teachers Institute published this effective overview of the Industrial Revolution: http://www.yale.edu/ynhti/curriculum/units/1981/2/81.02.06.x.html. Additionally, videos and images from this time period are effective resources. Photographer Lewis Hine famously captured images from this time period and included people and landscapes affected by the rise of industry. Many of his images can be found here: http://ehstoday.com/galleries/photographs-lewis-hine-industrial-revolution-and-child-laborers-photo-gallery#slide-0-field_images-31331.

- The Great Acceleration: Wendy Broadgate of the Future Earth blog offers a useful overview of the Great Acceleration and provides additional resources related directly to the connections between this period and the Anthropocene Epoch (http://www.futureearth.org/blog/2015-jan-16/great-acceleration). Additionally, this brief video (7 mins) offers an overview of the Great Acceleration that may be useful to students: https://www.youtube.com/watch?v=FVwrbEfd32o.

- The Information Age: This Prezi provides a basic but effective summary of the Information Age (https://prezi.com/qhaiddwj77l1/information-age-inventions/). In addition to providing information, the Prezi format may also give students ideas in developing their presentation to the textbook publishers.

- An interesting blog forum on the future of agriculture in the Information Age (https://www.oxfam.org/en/campaigns/future-agriculture-debate-experts).

NATIONAL SCIENCE TEACHING ASSOCIATION

Nature of Science/Nature of Historical Research Presentation Rubrics

	Expert	Competent	Emerging	Does Not Meet Expectations
Participation and Presentation	Student used time well focusing attention on the task. Appropriate communication (e.g. appropriate voice volume) was used throughout.	Student mostly used time well and stayed focused on the task, but student failed to adhere to appropriate communication expectations	Student lost focus on task at least once or failed to adhere to appropriate communication expectations	Student lost focus more than once, or failed on more than once occasion to use modest voice volume, or student was uncooperative about participating.
Content	Information on how researchers conduct their research was accurate and detailed. Information presented in an easy to understand manner.	Both *how* and *why* researchers use specific research techniques were discussed, but the presentation lacked detail.	How research is conducted is unclear, but the reason for using the research process is clear, or v/v.	Information given was lacking key information and difficult to understand.
Graphics	Graphic representation was neat and directly pertinent to content.	Graphic representation was neat and easy to understand.	Graphic representation was either messy or hard to understand.	Graphic representation was messy and hard to understand.

Graphic Organizer

Use this tool with your group to decide which period in human history should serve as the beginning marker for the Anthropocene Epoch.

Time Period/Event	Characteristics	Evidence Used	Ranking (1=most likely boundary, 6=least likely)
Birth of Agriculture			
Age of Exploration			
Industrial Revolution			
Great Acceleration			
Information Age			
Other			

Figure 4.2. Engineering Design Process

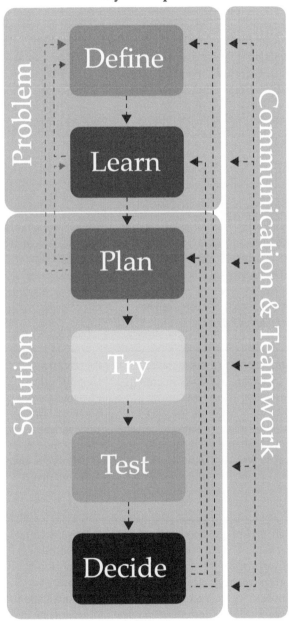

Copyright © 2015 PictureSTEM-Purdue University Research Foundation

Presentation Rubric

	Expert	Competent	Emerging	Did not Meet Expectations	Score
Evidence of Research Base	All content throughout the presentation is accurate. There are no factual errors. Clear evidence of research conducted and synthesized.	Most of the content is accurate but there is one piece of information that might be inaccurate. Evidence of research conducted, but limited synthesis is evident.	Content is generally accurate but there are several inconsistencies. Evidence of research conducted, but no synthesis is evident.	Little or no effort to present accurate content. Little evidence of research conducted, and no synthesis is evident.	
Content	Information is organized in a clear, logical way. It is easy to anticipate the type of material that might be on the next slide.	Most information is organized in a clear, logical way. One slide or item of information seems out of place.	Some information is logically sequenced. An occasional slide or item of information seems out of place.	There is no clear plan for the organization of information.	
Presentation	Presentation flows smoothly. All presenters are involved relatively equally and presentation adheres to time frame	Presentation flows smoothly. Presenters are involved relatively equally. Presentation is either over or under expected time frame	Presentation is choppy at times. Presenters are not all involved substantively. Presentation is either over or under expected time frame.	Presentation is choppy throughout. Presenters are not all involved substantively. Presentation is greatly over or under expected time frame.	
Recommendations	Excellent summary of topic with sound and feasible recommendations that impact audience. Introduces no new information.	Good summary of topic with clear concluding ideas and recommendations. Introduces no new information.	Basic summary of topic with some final concluding ideas and one recommendation. Introduces no new information.	Lack of summary of topic. No recommendations	

NATIONAL SCIENCE TEACHING ASSOCIATION

	Expert	Competent	Emerging	Did not Meet Expectations	Score
Collaboration	Presentation is clearly developed with international partners as evidenced by inclusion of all partners' perspectives in data and recommendations	Presentation is developed with International partners as evidenced by some inclusion of partners' perspectives in data and recommendations	Limited evidence of collaboration between partners in the presentation. Data presented and recommendations are largely from one perspective	Little or no evidence of collaboration between partners in the presentation. Data presented and recommendations are only from one perspective	

Textbook Entry Rubric

	Expert	Competent	Emerging	Did not Meet Expectation	Score
Introduction/ Thesis	Exceptional introduction that grabs interest of reader and states topic. Thesis is exceptionally clear, arguable, well developed, and a definitive statement.	Proficient introduction that is interesting and states topic. Thesis is a clear and arguable statement of position.	Basic introduction that states topic but lacks interest. Thesis is somewhat clear and arguable.	Weak or no introduction of topic. Paper's purpose is unclear/thesis is weak or missing.	
Quality of Information/ Evidence	Paper is exceptionally researched, extremely detailed, and information provided is accurate. Information clearly relates to the thesis.	Information relates to the main topic. Paper is well researched in detail and from a variety of sources.	Information relates to the main topic, few details and/ or examples are given. Shows a limited variety of sources.	Information has little or nothing to do with the thesis. Information has weak or no connection to the thesis.	
Support of Thesis/ Analysis	Exceptionally critical, relevant and consistent connections made between evidence and thesis. Excellent analysis.	Consistent connections made between evidence and thesis Good analysis.	Some connections made between evidence and thesis. Some analysis.	Limited or no connections made between evidence and thesis. Lack of analysis.	
Organization/ Development of Thesis	Exceptionally clear, logical, mature, and thorough development of thesis with excellent transitions between and within paragraphs.	Clear and logical order that supports thesis with good transitions between and within paragraphs.	Somewhat clear and logical development with basic transitions between and within paragraphs.	Lacks development of ideas with weak or no transitions between and within paragraphs.	

	Expert	Competent	Emerging	Did not Meet Expectation	Score
Conclusion and Recommendations	Excellent summary of topic with sound and feasible recommendations that impact reader. Introduces no new information.	Good summary of topic with clear concluding ideas and recommendations. Introduces no new information.	Basic summary of topic with some final concluding ideas and one recommendation. Introduces no new information.	Lack of summary of topic. No recommendations	
Collaboration	Paper is clearly written with partners as evidenced by inclusion of all partners' perspectives in data and recommendations	Paper is written with international partners as evidenced by some inclusion of partners' perspectives in data and recommendations	Limited evidence of collaboration between partners in the paper. Data presented and recommendations are largely from one perspective	Little or no evidence of collaboration between partners in the paper. Data presented and recommendations are only from one perspective	
Grammar/Usage/Mechanics	Control of grammar, usage, and mechanics. Almost entirely free of spelling, punctuation, and grammatical errors.	May contain few spelling, punctuation, and grammar errors.	Contains several spelling, punctuation, and grammar errors that detract from the paper's readability.	So many spelling, punctuation, and grammar errors that the paper cannot be understood.	

REFERENCES

Peters-Burton, E. E., Seshaiyer, P., Burton, S. R., Drake-Patrick, J., and Johnson, C. C. 2015. The STEM road map for grades 9–12. In C. C. Johnson, E. E. Peters-Burton, and T. J. Moore (Eds.), *STEM road map: A framework for integrated STEM education* (pp. 124–162). New York, NY: Routledge.

5

TRANSFORMING LEARNING WITH FORMATION OF THE EARTH AND THE *STEM ROAD MAP CURRICULUM SERIES*

Carla C. Johnson

This chapter serves as a conclusion to the Formation of the Earth integrated STEM curriculum module, but it is just the beginning of the transformation of your classroom that is possible through use of the *STEM Road Map Curriculum Series*. In this book, many key resources have been provided to make learning meaningful for your students through integration of science, technology, engineering, and mathematics, as well as social studies and English language arts, into powerful problem- and project-based instruction. First, the Formation of the Earth curriculum is grounded in the latest theory of learning for students in grade 9 specifically. Second, as your students work through this module, they engage in using the engineering design process (EDP) and build prototypes like engineers and STEM professionals in the real world. Third, students acquire important knowledge and skills grounded in national academic standards in mathematics, English language arts, science, and 21st century skills that will enable their learning to be deeper, retained longer, and applied throughout, illustrating the critical connections within and across disciplines. Finally, authentic formative assessments, including strategies for differentiation and addressing misconceptions, are embedded within the curriculum activities.

The Formation of the Earth curriculum in the Cause and Effect STEM Road Map theme can be used in single-content classrooms (e.g., mathematics) where there is only one teacher or expanded to include multiple teachers and content areas across classrooms. Through the exploration of the Era of Humans (Anthropocene), students engage in a real-world STEM problem on the first day of instruction and gather necessary knowledge and skills along the way in the context of solving the problem.

The other topics in the *STEM Road Map Curriculum Series* are designed in a similar manner, and NSTA Press and Routledge have published additional volumes in this series for this and other grade levels, and have plans to publish more.

DOI: 10.4324/9781003261766-7

For an up-to-date list of volumes in the series, please visit https://www.routledge.com/STEM-Road-Map-Curriculum-Series/book-series/SRM (for titles co-published by Routledge and NSTA Press), or https://www.nsta.org/book-series/stem-road-map-curriculum (for titles published by NSTA Press).

If you are interested in professional development opportunities focused on the STEM Road Map specifically or integrated STEM or STEM programs and schools overall, contact the lead editor of this project, Dr. Carla C. Johnson, Professor of Science Education at NC State University (carlacjohnson@ncsu.edu). Someone from the team will be in touch to design a program that will meet your individual, school, or district needs.

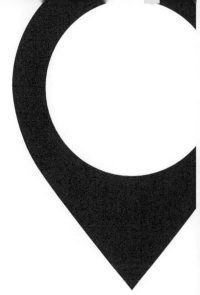

APPENDIX

CONTENT STANDARDS ADDRESSED IN STEM ROAD MAP MODULE

Table A.1. Next Generation Science Standards (NGSS)

Performance Expectations	Disciplinary Core Ideas and Crosscutting Concepts	Science and Engineering Practices
HS-LS2-1 Use mathematical and/or computational representations to support explanationsof factors that affect carrying capacity of ecosystemsat different scales. HS-LS2-2 Use mathematical representations to support and revise explanations based on evidenceabout factors affecting biodiversity and populations in ecosystemsof different scales. HS-ESS1-6 Apply scientific reasoning and evidencefrom ancient Earth materials, meteorites, and other planetary surfacesto construct an account of Earth's formationand early history. HS-ESS2-1 Develop a model to illustrate howEarth's internal and surface processes operate at different spatial andtemporal scalesto form continental and ocean-floor features. HS-ESS2-2 Analyze geoscience data to make the claim thatone change to Earth's surfacecan create feedbacksthat cause changes to other Earth systems. HS-ESS2-7 Construct an argument based on evidence aboutthe simultaneous coevolutionof Earth's systems and life on Earth. HS-ESS3-1 Construct an explanation based on evidence for howthe occurrence of natural hazards and changes in climatehave influenced human activity.	**Disciplinary Core Ideas** LS2.A: Interdependent Relationships in Ecosystems Ecosystems have carrying capacities, which are limits to the numbers of organisms and populations they can support. These limits result from such factors as the availability of living and nonliving resources and from such challenges such as predation, competition, and disease. Organisms would have the capacity to produce populations of great size were it not for the fact that environments and resources are finite. This fundamental tension affects the abundance (number of individuals) of species in any given ecosystem. LS2.C: Ecosystem Dynamics, Functioning, and Resilience A complex set of interactions within an ecosystem can keep its numbers and types of organisms relatively constant over long periods of time under stable conditions. If a modest biological or physical disturbance to an ecosystem occurs, it may return to its more or less original status (i.e., the ecosystem is resilient), as opposed to becoming a very different ecosystem. Extreme fluctuations in conditions or the size of any population, however, can challenge the functioning of ecosystems in terms of resources and habitat availability.	*Using Mathematics and Computational Thinking* Mathematical and computational thinking in 9-12 builds on K-8 experiences and progresses to using algebraic thinking and analysis, a range of linear and nonlinear functions including trigonometric functions, exponentials and logarithms, and computational tools for statistical analysis to analyze, represent, and model data. Simple computational simulations are created and used based on mathematical models of basic assumptions. Use mathematical and/or computational representations of phenomena or design solutions to support explanations. *Developing and Using Models* Modeling in 9–12 builds on K–8 experiences and progresses to using, synthesizing, and developing models to predict and show relationships among variables between systems and their components in the natural and designed world(s). Develop a model based on evidence to illustrate the relationships between systems or between components of a system.

Performance Expectations	Disciplinary Core Ideas and Crosscutting Concepts	Science and Engineering Practices
	ESS1.C: The History of Planet Earth Although active geologic processes, such as plate tectonics and erosion, have destroyed or altered most of the very early rock record on Earth, other objects in the solar system, such as lunar rocks, asteroids, and meteorites, have changed little over billions of years. Studying these objects can provide information about Earth's formation and early history. ESS2.A: Earth Materials and Systems Earth's systems, being dynamic and interacting, cause feedback effects that can increase or decrease the original changes. ESS2.B: Plate Tectonics and Large-Scale System Interactions Plate tectonics is the unifying theory that explains the past and current movements of the rocks at Earth's surface and provides a framework for understanding its geologic history. Plate movements are responsible for most continental and ocean-floor features and for the distribution of most rocks and minerals within Earth's crust. (ESS2.B Grade 8 GBE) ESS2.D: Weather and Climate The foundation for Earth's global climate systems is the electromagnetic radiation from the sun, as well as its reflection, absorption, storage, and redistribution among the atmosphere, ocean, and land systems, and this energy's re-radiation into space.	*Constructing Explanations and Designing Solutions* Constructing explanations and designing solutions in 9–12 builds on K–8 experiences and progresses to explanations and designs that are supported by multiple and independent student-generated sources of evidence consistent with scientific ideas, principles, and theories. Apply scientific reasoning to link evidence to the claims to assess the extent to which the reasoning and data support the explanation or conclusion. Construct an explanation based on valid and reliable evidence obtained from a variety of sources (including students' own investigations, models, theories, simulations, peer review) and the assumption that theories and laws that describe the natural world operate today as they did in the past and will continue to do so in the future. *Analyzing and Interpreting Data* Analyzing data in 9–12 builds on K–8 experiences and progresses to introducing more detailed statistical analysis, the comparison of data sets for consistency, and the use of models to generate and analyze data. Analyze data using tools, technologies, and/or models (e.g., computational, mathematical) in order to make valid and reliable scientific claims or determine an optimal design solution.

Continued

Table A.1. (*continued*)

Performance Expectations	Disciplinary Core Ideas and Crosscutting Concepts	Science and Engineering Practices
	PS1.C: Nuclear Processes Spontaneous radioactive decays follow a characteristic exponential decay law. Nuclear lifetimes allow radiometric dating to be used to determine the ages of rocks and other materials. (secondary) **Crosscutting Concepts** *Scale, Proportion, and Quantity* The significance of a phenomenon is dependent on the scale, proportion, and quantity at which it occurs. *Scale, Proportion, and Quantity* Using the concept of orders of magnitude allows one to understand how a model at one scale relates to a model at another scale. *Stability and Change* Much of science deals with constructing explanations of how things change and how they remain stable. *Cause and Effect* Empirical evidence is required to differentiate between cause and correlation and make claims about specific causes and effects. *Connections to Nature of Science* Scientific Knowledge is Open to Revision in Light of New Evidence Most scientific knowledge is quite durable, but is, in principle, subject to change based on new evidence and/or reinterpretation of existing evidence.	*Engaging in Argument from Evidence* Engaging in argument from evidence in 9–12 builds on K–8 experiences and progresses to using appropriate and sufficient evidence and scientific reasoning to defend and critique claims and explanations about the natural and designed world(s). Arguments may also come from current scientific or historical episodes in science. Construct an oral and written argument or counter-arguments based on data and evidence.

Performance Expectations	Disciplinary Core Ideas and Crosscutting Concepts	Science and Engineering Practices
	ESS2.E Biogeology The many dynamic and delicate feedbacks between the biosphere and other Earth systems cause a continual co-evolution of Earth's surface and the life that exists on it. ESS3.A: Natural Resources Resource availability has guided the development of human society. ESS3.B: Natural Hazards Natural hazards and other geologic events have shaped the course of human history; [they] have significantly altered the sizes of human populations and have driven human migrations. Science Models, Laws, Mechanisms, and Theories Explain Natural Phenomena A scientific theory is a substantiated explanation of some aspect of the natural world, based on a body of facts that have been repeatedly confirmed through observation and experiment and the science community validates each theory before it is accepted. If new evidence is discovered that the theory does not accommodate, the theory is generally modified in light of this new evidence. Models, mechanisms, and explanations collectively serve as tools in the development of a scientific theory *Connections to Engineering, Technology, and Applications of Science* Influence of Science, Engineering, and Technology on Society and the Natural World Modern civilization depends on major technological systems.	

Table A.2. Common Core Mathematics and English Language Arts (ELA) Standards

Common Core Mathematics	Common Core English/Language Arts (ELA)
Mathematics Practices MP1 Make sense of problems and persevere in solving them. MP3 Construct viable arguments and critique the reasoning of others. MP5 Use appropriate tools strategically. MP6 Attend to precision. MP8 Look for and express regularity in repeated reasoning. **Mathematics Content** HSN. RN.A.1 Explain how the definition of the meaning of rational exponents follows from extending the properties of integer exponents to those values, allowing for a notation for radicals in terms of rational exponents. HSN.Q.A.1 Use units as a way to understand problems and to guide the solution of multi-step problems; choose and interpret units consistently in formulas; choose and interpret the scale and the origin in graphs and data displays. HSN-Q.A.2 Define appropriate quantities for the purpose of descriptive modeling. HSS-ID.A.1 Represent data with plots on the real number line.	**Reading Standards** RI.9-10.1 Cite strong and thorough textual evidence to support analysis of what the text says explicitly as well as inferences drawn from the text. RI.9-10.2 Determine a central idea of a text and analyze its development over the course of the text, including how it emerges and is shaped and refined by specific details; provide an objective summary of the text. RI.9-10.7 Analyze various accounts of a subject told in different mediums (e.g., a person's life story in both print and multimedia), determining which details are emphasized in each account. RI.9-10.8 Delineate and evaluate the argument and specific claims in a text, assessing whether the reasoning is valid and the evidence is relevant and sufficient; identify false statements and fallacious reasoning. RI.9-10.10 By the end of grade 9, read and comprehend literacy nonfiction in the grades 9-10 text complexity band proficiently, with scaffolding as needed at the high end of the range. **Writing Standards** W.9-10.1a Introduce precise claim(s), distinguish the claim(s) from alternate or opposing claims, and create an organization that establishes clear relationships among claim(s), counterclaims, reasons, and evidence. W.9-10.1b Develop claim(s) and counterclaims fairly, supplying evidence for each while pointing out the strengths and limitations of both in a manner that anticipates the audience's knowledge level and concerns. W.9-10.1c Use words, phrases, and clauses to link the major sections of the text, create cohesion, and clarify the relationships between claim(s) and reasons, between reasons and evidence, and between claim(s) and counterclaims.

Common Core Mathematics	Common Core English/Language Arts (ELA)
	W.9-10.1d Establish and maintain a formal style and objective tone while attending to the norms and conventions of the discipline in which they are writing. W.9-10.1e Provide a concluding statement or section that follows from and supports the argument presented. W.9-10.2a Introduce a topic; organize complex ideas, concepts, and information to make important connections and distinctions; include formatting (e.g., headings), graphics (e.g., figures, tables), and multimedia when useful to aiding comprehension. W.9-10.2b Develop the topic with well-chosen, relevant, and sufficient facts, extended definitions, concrete details, quotations, or other information and examples appropriate to the audience's knowledge of the topic. W.9-10.2c Use appropriate and varied transitions to link the major sections of the text, create cohesion, and clarify the relationships among complex ideas and concepts. W.9-10.2d Use precise language and domain-specific vocabulary to manage the complexity of the topic. W.9-10.2e Establish and maintain a formal style and objective tone while attending to the norms and conventions of the discipline in which they are writing. W.9-10.2f Provide a concluding statement or section that follows from and supports the information or explanation presented (e.g., articulating implications or the significance of the topic). W.9-10.4 Produce clear and coherent writing in which the development, organization, and style are appropriate to task, purpose, and audience. W.9-10.6 Use technology, including the Internet, to produce, publish, and update individual or shared writing products, taking advantage of technology's capacity to link to other information and to display information flexibly and dynamically.

Continued

Formation of the Earth, Grade 9

Table A.2. (*continued*)

Common Core Mathematics	Common Core English/Language Arts (ELA)
	W.9-10.8 Gather relevant information from multiple authoritative print and digital sources, using advanced searches effectively; assess the usefulness of each source in answering the research question; integrate information into the text selectively to maintain the flow of ideas, avoiding plagiarism and following a standard format for citation.
	W.9-10.10 Write routinely over extended time frames (time for research, reflection, and revision) and shorter time frames (a single sitting or a day or two) for a range of tasks, purposes, and audiences.
	Speaking and Listening Standards
	SL.9-10.1 Initiate and participate effectively in a range of collaborative discussions (one-on-one, in groups, and teacher-led) with diverse partners on grades 9-10 topics, texts, and issues, building on others' ideas and expressing their own clearly and persuasively.
	SL.9-10.2 Integrate multiple sources of information presented in diverse media or formats (e.g., visually, quantitatively, orally) evaluating the credibility and accuracy of each source.
	SL.9-10.4 Present information, findings, and supporting evidence clearly, concisely, and logically such that listeners can follow the line of reasoning and the organization, development, substance, and style are appropriate to purpose, audience, and task.
	SL.9-10.5 Make strategic use of digital media (e.g., textual, graphical, audio, visual, and interactive elements) in presentations to enhance understanding of findings, reasoning, and evidence and to add interest.
	SL.9-10.6 Adapt speech to a variety of contexts and tasks, demonstrating command of formal English when indicated or appropriate.

Common Core Mathematics	Common Core English/Language Arts (ELA)
	Language Standards L.9-10.2 Demonstrate command of the conventions of standard English capitalization, punctuation, and spelling when writing. L.9-10.6 Acquire and use accurately general academic and domain-specific words and phrases, sufficient for reading, writing, speaking, and listening at the college and career readiness level; demonstrate independence in gathering vocabulary knowledge when considering a word or phrase important to comprehension or expression.

Table A.3. 21st Century Skills Addressed in STEM Road Map Module

21st Century Skills	Learning Skills and Technology Tools (from P21 framework)	Teaching Strategies	Evidence of Success
21st century interdisciplinary themes	Global Awareness Civic Literacy Environmental Literacy	Teachers will direct student attention towards connections between various eras, periods, and epochs that have come and gone in the formation of the Earth. Through this study, students will learn about how various scientific disciplines including biology, chemistry and geology inform each other. Study of these fields will further inform how humans' impact on the Earth has shaped the planet.	Students will develop a robust understanding of how the Earth has formed, the attributes and delineations of eras, periods, and epochs and demonstrate this knowledge in a multimodal presentation where they apply conceptual understanding to the current geologic period.

Continued

Table A.3. (*continued*)

21st Century Skills	Learning Skills and Technology Tools (from P21 framework)	Teaching Strategies	Evidence of Success
Learning and innovation skills	Creativity and Innovation Critical Thinking and Problem Solving Communication and Collaboration	Teachers will offer access to resources related to how the Earth formed and the ways geologists address questions of time periods and time period transitions in their study of the Earth's formation. Additionally, teachers will guide students in problem solving strategies to support the work of groups to identify challenges and develop means to address these challenges.	Students will collaborate with partners to develop a multimodal presentation dedicated to sharing their understanding of the Earth's formation and how our current period has been shaped by humankind. Through this presentation, student groups will share findings of their work to identify themes related to Earth's eras, periods, and epochs. This effort will also include work to communicate connections and themes they find in order to communicate with a textbook company interested in including a section of dedicated to the Anthropocene Epoch.
Information, media and technology skills	Information Literacy Media Literacy ICT Literacy	Teachers will require the use of different reliable sources for this project and challenge students to share their work through a multimodal presentation they develop to share with a mock textbook publishing company	Students will use a variety of reliable sources and cite these resources accordingly in their final products, which will be shared in part through a presentation developed and shared by the student groups to assist textbook publishers regarding whether and how to include the Anthropocene Epoch in textbooks. Evidence of success will also include a publication-ready multimedia textbook passage describing the Anthropocene Epoch.
Life and career skills	Flexibility and Adaptability Initiative and Self-Direction Social and Cross Cultural Skills Productivity and Accountability Leadership and Responsibility	Teachers will provide check points for students to self-monitor their progress at each of the phases of the project.	Students will articulate their goals for each check point for the project and devise strategic plans to show progress toward their goals. Students will work effectively in collaborative groups and be clear about roles of each member.

Table A.4. English Language Development Standards Addressed in STEM Road Map Module

English Language Development Standards: Grades 9-12 (WIDA, 2012)
ELD Standard 1: Social and Instructional Language
English language learners communicate for social and instructional purposes within the school setting.
ELD Standard 2: The Language of Language Arts
English language learners communicate information, ideas, and concepts necessary for academic success in the content area of language arts.
ELD Standard 3: The Language of Mathematics
English language learners communicate information, ideas, and concepts necessary for academic success in the content area of mathematics
ELD Standard 4: The Language of Science.
English language learners communicate information, ideas, and concepts necessary for academic success in the content area of science
ELD Standard 5: The Language of Social Studies
English language learners communicate information, ideas, and concepts necessary for academic success in the content area of social studies.

INDEX

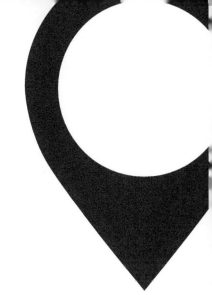

Note: Page numbers in **bold** type refer to tables
Page numbers in *italic* type refer to figures

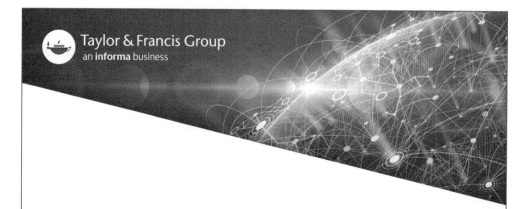